The Spirit of Canoe Camping

A Handbook for Wilderness Canoeists

Harry Drabik

illustrated by Randall Scholes

Acknowledgement to Rudolph Carlson for Illustration of Canoe Stroke Drawings. Also thanks to Chuck Wechlsler for all his help!

4th Printing 1988

ISBN-0-931714-11-7

Nodin Press, a division of Micawber's, Inc.
525 North Third Street,
Minneapolis, MN 55401

Printed in U.S.A. at McNaughton & Gunn, Inc., Saline, MI

To my parents, who got me started, and Cliff Kippley, Scoutmaster, who started more than either of us realized when he got me to go camping.

About the Author

Harry Drabik, a native of Chicago, came to northern Minnesota as a boy. That was the beginning of a love affair with the Upper Lake Superior and Canoe Country region. Work in education and the outdoors all contributed to the formation of a new wilderness program and ethic.

In 1974 the idea for Pigeon River Expeditions was born and eventually became the first private Outfitter-Guide for the Superior National Forest, including the BWCA.

This book has grown out of Pigeon River Expeditions and is based on real experiences with people. Pigeon River Expeditions operates out of Hovland, Box 547, Minnesota 55606.

Table of Contents

Introduction

This is a book about wilderness-style canoe camping. Most of the experience behind it was gained in the Boundary Waters Canoe Area Wilderness, but the style of camping is something common to many other areas.

Canoe camping is relaxing and easy enough for a variety of people. You don't have to be a marvelous athlete. Wilderness areas are places where people can enjoy the simple life, like canoe camping. The simplicity of it makes it easy. It's my hope that more families will begin to take advantage of the opportunity. This book is written with that objective in mind.

"Can I take my kids on a wilderness trip?" is a question I hear often. My answer is, yes, definitely! This book will give you tips on how to prepare for an outing, and what to expect. Because canoe camping is basic, it fits a wide variety of ages and abilities. There is something for nearly everyone. I'm not aware of any stage in life where moderate exercise, fresh air, nature, and companionship can't be worked in. Kids, in particular, seem to thrive on it.

You may find that your family, alone, lacks the proper balance for a trip. It takes two adults or responsible teens for every younger child. However, a family trip need not stop with family members. Two families can pool together, or relatives, friends, neighbors, etc. You probably know someone you'd like to know better. Why not see if they are interested? If you appreciate someone's character, humor, or wisdom, you have a candidate worth asking. Many people would be pleased, flattered, or appreciative of an invitation.

"Can we afford it?" is another common question. Again, the answer is yes. Some wilderness-type activity and equipment is costly. What's described here isn't expensive.

In most cases, a family can own two canoes for the price of a new outboard motor. The canoes can be cartopped, and the cost of a boat and trailer is saved. You won't be towing anything, so travel on the road is safer and more economical. This use of more flexible equipment may even get you out for more weekends close to home. So, it is likely that your recreational money will go further.

If you rent equipment, you'll find the cost of renting comparable to other vacations you've taken. In most cases, you can save money by providing some of your own equipment. So, there are options in renting that may be just right for your budget or your means of transportation.

"What kind of shape do I have to be in?" is another frequent question. If you lead an average life at work and home, most likely you are fit enough. A wilderness trip won't make you less fit. If you camp with a group which is tolerant, relaxed, and patient, then athletic ability won't make much difference. Attitude is more important. So long as we try, learn, and cooperate, wilderness is an understanding master.

People with physical disabilities, the elderly, or the very young can be right at home on a moderate wilderness trip. Cooperation from one another and a lesser amount of travel will make it possible. A trip need not be a contest of endurance or mileage. The value of wilderness experience isn't measured in portages and paddling speed. Your experience will be just as valid if you see 4 lakes or 40.

It isn't dumb for people to inquire or even have doubts about something they've never done before, or did long ago. First camping experiences are often pretty ragged, and the idea of going into "wilderness" sounds too ambitious. I don't blame anyone for being skeptical or cautious. That's a good trait; people like that will make wise wilderness campers.

I've been active in camping for most of my adult life. Since I established Pigeon River Expeditions. I've introduced many people to wilderness canoe camping. It's not complicated. It's mostly a matter of basic camping and canoeing skills. The rest is enjoyment. I've had people ranging from toddlers to near-80 on canoe trips. I know it can be done. I hope more people will grasp the opportunity for human activity and growth that is part of wilderness travel.

When I wrote this book, I wanted it to be practical. I think it is. You see, I have to keep camping simple and practical or I'd go crazy. I just couldn't keep it up week after week if it got to be a monumental task. I try to keep my feet on the ground, and as far as I know, that's still the best way to walk or live.

"Why is a 'practical' book called The Spirit Of Canoe Camping?" This book consists of two parts. The first half is the 'practical' part. That's where you'll find specific information about equipment, skills, techniques, etc. It deals with camping and canoeing basics, each chapter building on information in preceding chapters.

You'll notice that the chapter on Canoe Trip Plans comes toward the end of the practical section. It's not out of place. It belongs there because a good plan is based on a background of information and experience. Planning is the most complex task, because it takes in the greatest area.

The second part of the book deals with experience. That's where the 'spirit' comes in. Wilderness travel is more than exercise. Being re-acquainted with nature and human values is part of the experience.

You see, we are in the spirit of things when we live together, seeking peace and harmony. Some situation may frustrate us, but we can bounce back and give the best that's in us. On a day when the portages are steep and slippery, the value of a helping hand and a smile are crystal clear.

We are in the spirit of things when we see the beauty of a natural environment. It's more than any of us can understand, but it's not more than we can appreciate or enjoy. Nature refreshes the spirit—it's something we can hold to. Experience in nature lives within us.

We are in the spirit of things when we discover that a canoe trip is like time travel. Science hasn't solved the time barrier, but you can come close. Each trip is a step into a different relationship between man and nature. We go back to a way of living and travel that is as old as man. It's a good time and place for gaining perspective.

I could write volumes about the spirit of canoe camping. But the spirit of it and the experience is really something for *you* to capture. That's what awaits you. I can only tell you that every trip, great or small, begins and ends with the basics of camping. It's the best place to start, and it's the way that will carry you farthest.

Philosophy Of Camping

People have often asked me, *"What is meant by wilderness camping?"* My answer is that wilderness camping is not an escape from civilization, but a simplification of the civilized world. The tent is your house, the campfire your kitchen stove, the canoe your vehicle for transportation and outdoor fun.

Wilderness camping gets us back to basics. Society, too, is simplified to the acts of several people who must get along, share, and work together for obvious, survival-related reasons. Sharing basic duties helps us to see that living and working together can be fun; that's the human reason for camping. It brings us face to face with what we need, in material and human terms, to be functional human beings. The connection between function and fun becomes clear.

Camping simplfies civilization. That should tell us something: Keep Your Plans And Equipment Simple.

Get rid of the clutter. Enjoy simplicity and the company of people. Live simply and well. I chuckle to myself about the expensive and elaborate things I've done to put some spark in my life. Those efforts did some good, but they were costly in terms of cash and stress. Wilderness is easy on the budget, and it eases stress as only nature can.

Some people approach wilderness with a 'conquest of nature' attitude. I suppose that's OK. I prefer to accept nature as it is, however that might be. I don't expect a string of sunny days. It's easier to accept the outdoors for what it is, mosquitoes included. If you are out to fight or conquer nature, you are going into camping with a hostile attitude. Nature has no plans either for or against you. There is no challenge, no contest, no domination. The door to the outdoors opens most easily with the key of acceptance. Learning that is an important step.

I have some rules, if that's the right word, to help me keep my approach simple and realistic.

1. Keep it Safe. Do not over-extend yourself. Do not take risks that can be avoided; that's what survival is all about. Be careful of fatigue; be wise enough to rest. If you are aware of your physical and mental needs, you will be able to accept your human limits.

2. Keep It Repeatable. Your practices should be simple and effective enough so you can repeat tomorrow and the next day what you did today. In other words, you could paddle over 30 miles in one day, but do you want to repeat that for a week? Keep your pace and thinking within reason. Camping is a human adventure, not a superhuman effort. Reasonable camping has enough flex so people can bounce back, even if the going gets rough.

3. Keep It Considerate. Be considerate of others in your party, of other

groups, and of nature. Help when people need help. Learn and work together. A good suggestion may come from anyone. Leave your campsite in order. Keep your voice down and your spirit up.

These rules help me to enjoy and appreciate the outdoors. Another way to enhance your camping trip is to learn something about the area where you'll be camping. Read about its history, its birds, mammals, plants, and geology. Then allow time during your trip to enjoy these things. Hide your canoe in the reeds and watch for ducks. From an overlook, watch beaver at work in their pond. If you are in a hurry, you'll miss many of nature's offerings.

Camping and being close to nature is an old tradition. For ages, it was our way of life. The ancients survived by sharing, by accepting nature, and by using what was at hand. Modern people will find it requires time and effort to prepare body and soul for a wilderness experience. But it sure beats a quick spin that only skims the surface of our wilderness heritage.

I enjoy guiding more than anything I've done. But my personal goal is to put myself out of business. I try to teach people well enough so they don't need me any more. They can copy and use my techniques because I keep them simple and obvious. I have no secret practices or tricks. I didn't invent any of this; I have simply organized it a bit.

The job of experiencing, of sharing, of knowing the land is rightly yours. The wilderness heritage is yours to discover and yours to hold in trust. My job is to guide; I leave the important things for you.

Program and Recreation

Your program of activities on a canoe trip will depend on your interests and preparation. There are sources of information for wilderness areas. The National Park Service, U.S. Forest Service, state historical societies, and state departments of natural resources are excellent sources. Your public library can provide information, too.

Gather enough information so you can be realistically prepared for camping in an area. Research will tell you what to expect. It will help you adjust to and enjoy a place unfamiliar to you. But, no matter how promising or exciting an area seems, a camping trip still rests on basic skills. These are constant and needed every day. It helps to keep that in mind in every phase of planning.

Time is an important consideration as you plan your trip. If you are constantly in a rush to reach a planned destination, you won't have time to observe and enjoy what you come across.

For example, if you pass by a beaver dam or lodge during the day, return to it at dusk and watch for signs of activity. Beaver and other wildlife are active at twilight. Moose often feed on lily pads close to shore. Listen for the odd, musical hum from the wings of Nighthawks as the birds dive toward the water. A Nighthawk may be flying high over the lake, then swoop down to catch a moth flying inches above the water. Bats, using their gift of 'echo location', dart after insects flying over the lake. With luck, a deer may come into the open for water.

You have to put yourself near the right habitat at the right time. You won't see as much if you stay glued to your campsite all evening. At the very least, you can enjoy one of the best times of the day for a quiet paddle. There are fewer mosquitoes away from shore, and it's a good time to cast a lure or try some slow trolling. There is plenty to see and feel if you give yourself the time.

Swimming is a nice recreation, especially at the end of the day. You'll feel refreshed, and sleep better. A swim cools your body, and that makes you less attractive to insects. Swim with a concern for safety. Look out for one another; use the Buddy System.

You may want to wash up. Be sure to use a biodegradable soap. After getting wet, lather up on shore. If possible, have someone rinse you off by using a large cook kit pail. Try to keep soap from entering the water. Don't leave a bar of soap sitting by the water. It could get kicked in or forgotten. In most cases, it is possible to bathe some distance from camp, away from where you will draw drinking or cooking water. Be considerate of water quality and exercise moderation. Clean water isn't just nice, it's vital to a healthy outdoors.

Exploring is fun. If a trail crosses your portage, why not see where it goes? Why is there a clearing on that shore of the lake? Where did those big saw-logs come from? Is this the sort of campsite that was used in pre-historic times? Again, take the time to look around. The wild country has many stories and a few mysteries, but there are no bronze plaques to provide the answers.

To break the daily routine of paddling, why not climb into the higher country between lakes? The forest community is different on high ground, and the view can be superb. Or, paddle up a small creek that twists and turns through acres of marsh reeds alive with birds. Between lakes are swampy lands full of life; it's worth a short hike in such terrain. Each area has its own natural flavor. But, you won't discover them if you stick to the portages and main lakes.

Fishing can be enjoyable and useful on a canoe trip. I never plan on a meal of fish, but a mess of fillets can improve any meal. For convenience, we use pack rods with metal ferrules. Each rod is packed in a separate tube, while the reels are packed in separate pouches.

Fishing tackle can consist of two or three spoons, a few spinners, some hooks, ball-bearing swivels, assorted sinkers or split shot, and a few twister-type jigs. A small assortment is enough, and it can be packed easily. A plastic stringer is handy to have along. I have, at times, bent down the barbs on my hooks with a pliers so I can release smaller fish uninjured. This causes me to lose a few fish, but I feel better about the quality of my fishing.

Northern lakes aren't hard to fish, but a few techniques are worth mentioning. Try trolling as you paddle along a rocky shore. One canoe can troll a spoon and the other a jig. Good places to fish are wherever rivers enter or leave lakes. Other good places are pools below rapids or falls. Deep holes in narrow channels are worth a try. Islands and points with rocky reefs that drop off fast are often good.

The best time to fish is usually toward evening, but I never predict when fish will bite fastest. Don't keep more fish than you can eat that day or at breakfast the following morning. Without refrigeration, fish spoil quickly.

Another concern is fishing while travelling. Dragging fish on a stringer all day and carrying them over portages is a messy chore, and the fish will soon die. It is better to promptly release a fish in it's home waters than to have it spoil before you make camp.

After cleaning your catch, carry the remains inland, well away from water and your campsite. Don't be lazy about it. Also, rinse off the area where you cleaned your fish. Hornets, in particular, like to hang around places where fish were cleaned, and you don't want these pests around camp.

One other tip. If you are camped on a rocky shore at dusk, cast out a light-colored twister jig. Let it sink to the bottom. Retrieve the lure with slow jerks, like it was a crayfish darting from rock to rock. If it snags, have a canoe handy so you can go out to work it loose.

With patience and luck you may get a nice fish for breakfast. That pleasant opportunity, however, may backfire if you forget to check on the rules. Within twenty miles of my home there are three different licenses and sets of regulations; state, province, and Indian reservation. It pays to double check to see if you are fishing legally.

A book on nature identification, birds, etc. may be good to bring along. Similarly, a historical journal may be interesting to read and follow each day. You can search for that special piece of driftwood, or collect rocks. With a small amount of plaster you can take an animal track. And, there are many, many good photographs all around you. You can't possibly do all these things, so just take advantage of what comes along. It will be enough.

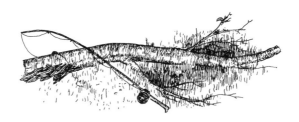

Clothing

Think of clothing as portable shelter. It does for you during the day what your tent and sleeping bag do at night. It protects you so you can conserve energy for basic functions and special interests. Exposure to sun, wind, insects, abrasion, water, etc., draws energy from your system, especially when you are not used to constant exposure. When you take into account the excitement of the trip, new situations, a different environment, well, it all adds up to a lot of physical adjustment which can effect your performance and enjoyment of the outdoors.

I usually specify a dark or light color for certain items of clothing. Dark colors pick up heat from the sun, and the fabric will dry quicker. So, wear darker clothing for those items that you want to dry quickly after getting wet or being washed. However, you don't want the upper part of your body to overheat, so wear light colors there.

I do not vary my list of personal equipment. Years of experience have taught me what I can rely on and what will work. Clothing is not something I take lightly; having the proper clothes has often made my outing more enjoyable.

What is the proper apparel for canoe camping? Here's what I wear and use every day.

Boots: I prefer six-inch high, unlined leather boots with flat or wedge soles. It's best if the eyelets go all the way up, instead of having hooks on the upper part. Hooks bend and catch in tall grass, but they can be replaced, cheaply, with speed lace rings. (The Irish Setter Sport Boot—No. 875-1 by Red Wing is excellent.)

In canoe country your feet will sometimes end up in the water; it can't be helped. Waterproof your boots by oiling them repeatedly, until they become oily to the touch. Hiking or Mountain type boots are not practical for canoe camping, and boots with lugged soles tear up trails and campsites. A flat sole is gentle on the earth, and clay will not build up under your heels as badly.

Socks: I wear long, dark-colored, wool and nylon blend, snowmobile-type socks. They are a bit warm for summer, but they cushion the foot on portages. The socks should come up to mid-calf, which helps keep insects from getting at your ankles. Don't use socks with tight elastic tops which reduce circulation.

Under Shorts: I prefer dark-colored nylon or cotton shorts. Nylon dries quicker, and it doesn't feel so clammy on a hot day. Fishnet shorts are not advised because of the amount of time spent sitting and paddling.

Trousers: I wear dark-colored work pants with no cuffs. My pants are cut so they just cover the tops of my boots. Shorter trousers don't get as wet when I step into shallow water or when the dew is heavy. I see no advantage in longer pants because the bottoms get wet and muddy. Blue jeans are among the slowest to dry; I never wear them camping.

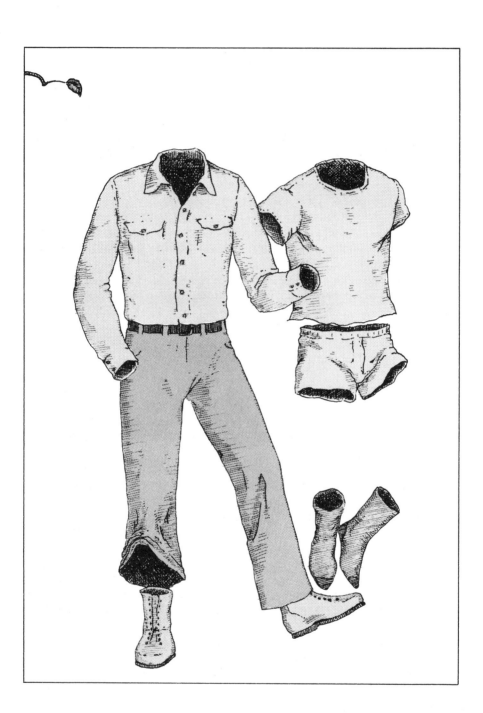

T-Shirt: I like a light-colored cotton T-Shirt. The light color is cooler, and if it is warm, I can wear either a regular shirt alone or just the T-Shirt. Mostly, I try to avoid too much exposure to the sun, insects, etc., (always wear a long-sleeved shirt on portages.) I avoid fishnet T-Shirts because they leave a pattern of small blood blisters in a waffle pattern where the pack straps ride.

Shirt: My favorite is a tan work shirt with long sleeves and two front pockets with button flaps. Shirt pockets with button flaps are good in the outdoors where a person frequently bends over to work. You don't want things to keep slipping out of your pockets. A light-colored shirt is cooler and more comfortable on warm days. Avoid blue shirts. Mosquitoes seem to be attracted to blue, possibly because blue picks up more heat from the sun.

Miscellaneous: I wear a strong leather belt and a folding belt knife in a sheath. I carry a folding stainless steel cup, by Yorkshire, Ltd., in my shirt pocket, because it is a good idea to replenish fluids lost through working. I have a dark-colored bandana in my pocket. The bandana is useful during strenuous activity and as a fly wisk. I often wear a hat, but I have yet to settle on any one style. A hat reduces exposure to the sun.

Avoid clothing and accessories that are gaudy, loud, or which 'advertise'. Such things are out of place in the bush.

In my personal pack, I carry one complete change of clothes which consists of everything already described. The following items also go into my personal pack.

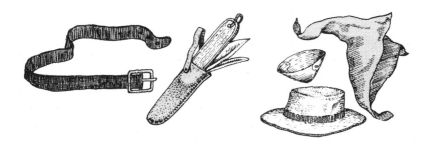

Jacket: I use a medium weight, woolen jac shirt with no tails. Wool will keep me warm even if it gets wet or damp. The jac shirt is also handy for keeping mosquitoes off in the evening; they'll land, but they can't penetrate the wool to feast. The jac shirt should have pockets with button flaps.

Swim Suit: I prefer a light nylon suit because it dries quickly. Swim suits should be hung to dry immediately after use. I pack the suit in a small plastic bag, and I carry a few spare bags with it. I never mix a wet or damp suit with dry clothing. A really wet suit should be carried in the pack pocket.

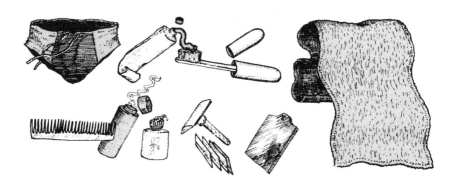

Towel And Grooming: I carry a dark-colored, medium weight towel. A tooth brush in a holder, tooth paste in a plastic bottle, stick deodorant, metal comb, stainless steel mirror, razor blades and razor are wrapped up in the towel, inside a plastic bag. A four-ounce bottle of sunburn lotion and a one-ounce bottle of insect repellent are included. I usually carry an additional one-ounce bottle of insect repellent in one of my pockets, where it is handy during the day.

A word on insect repellent. The active ingredient is N-diethylmeta-toluamide, called 'deet'. The highest percentage of this ingredient is found in the small bottles of cream or liquid repellent. Sprays and foams are bulky, less effective, and wasteful.

Rain Suit: I carry a two-piece, nylon rain suit. It is urethane coated and has sealed seams. It is a lightweight item, and somewhat expensive. This is one item that you will get exactly what you pay for. Good rain gear is expensive. Pick a simple design with no frills or gimmicks. It is silly to be adjusting a complicated rain suit in a downpour. The rain jacket should just cover your pants pockets. Some of the longer rain jackets are made for hikers, but when sitting in a canoe, you'll find them inconvenient. I use the rain jacket over my jac shirt when the weather is cool and windy. I carry the rain suit just under the flap of my personal pack, so I can get at it easily.

My clothing list does not mention items for women or children. Why? Because I don't feel comfortable recommending things which I have not tried myself. However, the basic principles put down here can be adapted for women or children with little trouble. They are: full body protection, comfort, durability, ease of drying, warmth, and versatility. These principles apply for any body, male or female, young or old.

Tents

As a child, my tents were private worlds: dark, usually hot, and smelling strongly of treated canvas. I frequently got wet and often ended up in ridiculously miserable situations. Over the years, I struggled with heavy canvas tents with sewn-in floors that would never dry. I tried floorless tents, using plastic sheeting for the floor. But, they always let in mosquitoes. I used big tents and small tents. I tried using just about anything I could get my hands on; later, I bought and experimented with various shelters that seemed promising.

For canoe camping, I look for the following in a tent.

It should be self-supporting. It should have an external aluminum framework with no center pole at the door. The design and shape should be simple, like an A-Frame. It should be nylon, with a sewn-in floor, a full fly, front and rear ventilation which can be closed, and some shock cording. It should have ample room for two people, which means a floor area about 7 x 9 feet. The nylon should be completely urethane coated, except for the roof area under the fly. The floor should be of the 'boat' type. It should have two D rings inside for a clothesline along the ridge, and it should have one or two pockets inside for glasses, etc. It should weigh no more than ten pounds.

Your tent should be a natural color. (I prefer green.) It should not be so costly that you will be afraid to use it. The tent should roll up into a bundle which fits into a case no larger than 7 inches in diameter by 28 inches long. The tent door should be shaped like an A, and it should zip down one side and fully across the bottom. The mosquito net should be the same as the door in shape. 'No-See-Um' netting is best.

My current choice, which fits all of the above, is the Eureka, Four Person, Timberline. It is an excellent tent, both summer and winter. The floor has two seams which **must** be sealed. (Eureka provides the sealant with each new tent), but other than that, it is easy to live with. It is also surprisingly strong and flexible.

Five years ago I was pinned down on a wilderness lake during a three-day storm. The second day was marked by severe wind gusts, and I saw at least one water-spout nearby. I was in my Eureka Timberline when it was lifted and moved by gale-force winds. Unbelievably, there was no damage to the tent, and it was quickly put back into position. On that day the tent did much better than my nerves, which were about shot. I still use that tent.

Your choice of a tent is, of course, yours. But for me, camping and tents should be simple. Tents much larger than 7 x 9 feet won't fit on many wilderness campsites because large, level spots are not common. Smaller tents will fit in tighter spots, but they do not offer as much convenient protection for people and equipment.

ILLUSTRATION SHOWS GROUND CLOTH EXPOSED. IN USE, GROUND CLOTH IS COVERED BY TENT.

The tent is a large and visible piece of equipment, but stop and think about what it does. Your tent keeps water, wind, and insects out. That's its purpose. Knowing that gives some clues as to how to use it.

Selecting the right location is important. Your campsite should provide some protection from the wind. The ground should be reasonably flat, with some ground cover. A bare earth site makes for messy, dirty camping, especially if it rains. A good site is away from the water, away from the full force of the wind, but exposed to enough breeze to keep insects away. A tree or two can screen the tent in a driving rain; such natural protection will complement your tent.

Before setting up your tent, first put down a ground cloth. The ground cloth is roughly the same size as the tent floor, so if the ground cloth fits the spot, so will the tent. The ground cloth protects the tent floor from abrasion, puncture by twigs, and from sticky pine sap. The floor is a critical wear area, and it deserves extra protection.

I'm currently using a 6 x 8 Versa Tarp under tents. The Versa Tarp is durable, waterproof, and light. The 6 x 8 size is just right for use under a 7 x 9 tent. If you use regular plastic under your tent, make sure it doesn't stick out beyond the tent floor. Fold it back before you erect the tent. If you allow the plastic to stick out, water can pocket between the tent floor and the ground cloth if it rains. That's like pitching your tent in a wading pool. Erecting and folding tents on the ground cloth helps to keep them clean and in good condition.

I always leave front and rear vents open six or eight inches when folding the tent. That helps air to escape from the tent during the folding and rolling. In addition, it enables you to set up faster because air can get back in. If the tent is in sunlight, I open the front flap wide. I put my gear, unpacked, in the tent, and leave the flap open until evening, when I close it to the damp night air. If left tightly closed during the day, tent will act like a condensor and some humidity (water) will form inside. The tent door should be rolled and tied along one side, but the screen should be zipped shut to keep insects out.

If it is raining when it comes time to pitch tents, wait awhile for the rain to slacken. While waiting, put up the rain tarp near the cooking area. A tent laid out flat will take in water during pitching and before the fly is in place. If it is raining hard, omit the ground cloth because it will hold water against the tent floor. After the tent is up, I use my towel to pick up any water inside the tent. Beyond that, I avoid going into the tent during a rain, until I am ready to retire for the night. A person in a dripping rain suit is like a small storm in a tent. At night, I keep the rain suit and other wet clothing by the door, away from the sleeping area.

Keep your tent and sleeping gear as free of water and humidity as possible. Keep wet towels, swim suits, etc. hung up outside. Try never to go into a tent with anything wet, even for a moment. If a tent is very wet, it should be allowed to dry out as much as possible before moving camp. You can shake some water off the tent, and you may wish to hang it off the ground so it can dry more completely and quickly. Drying is important because it reduces weight and makes for a more comfortable shelter. If you must move on with wet tents, try to stop early and set up a new camp while you still have some drying time.

If it rains at night, keep away from the side and end walls while sleeping. Water can be drawn through the fabric if you lay against a wall. Because of this, I use a four-person tent for two people. That arrangement allows two adults to sleep toward the center of the tent without being cramped for space. Sleeping bags slide easily on nylon tent floors, and you'll have to be alert to prevent sliding toward a wall.

If it is very windy, try to pitch your tent so one end, rather than a side, faces into the wind. That reduces strain on the tent. The toes and heels of boots also strain tent fabric. Usually, I remove my boots first when I retire for the night. The tent door and screen also take a lot of strain. Careful pitching will help, as will gentle use of zippers. The door and screen are important; pay close attention to the front of the tent so it is not stretched overly tight, straining the zippers.

I fold and store tents the same way each day and after each trip. I also examine each tent, and write down things that will need attention. Nylon repair tape followed by a coating of K Kote by Kenyon makes a good repair. A methodical approach will save you a lot of grief. But, equipment is only equipment; you have to do the thinking and exercise good care.

Sleeping Bags

Sleeping well is important to performing well and enjoying what the wild country offers. I find it is wise to let people sleep until they begin to rouse. That way, I know they are rested, and I much prefer rested people to tired, grouchy ones. Part of the secret of sleeping well is being warm and comfortable enough so your body can relax and not have to work so hard.

You should be aware of what happens each time you use your bag. At night, when the bag is spread out, it will pick up moisture from the night air. Additional moisture is given off by the body during the night. Some people cover their heads with the bag, so they breathe in even more moisture. After two nights, you can feel the moisure build up in a bag. It gets clammy.

Try to air your bag each morning, at least 15 minutes on each side. Open the bag and hang it in direct sunlight. I prefer bags with a slightly tapered shape and a dark color so they absorb heat from the sun. A full-length zipper, with top and bottom opening is best. Bags which can zip together are sometimes practical.

I stuff a sleeping bag into its sack starting at the bottom of the bag. Each stuffed bag then goes into a plastic sack; I carry a few spare plastic sacks in case a replacement is needed. Your sleeping bag **must** have this protection when you are not using or drying it. In rainy weather, I pack my bag as soon as I get up. A bag left spread out will absorb much more moisture than one which is packed away.

At night, I position the bag toward the center of the floor, away from the ends and sides of the tent. It is smart to always follow the same sleeping arrangement, just in case you awake suddenly to find things blowing away outside. If you use the same arrangement, you will know immediately the location of your flashlight, clothes, etc.

My pillow is the bag's stuff sack filled with spare clothes from the personal pack. I don't use clothes worn during the day for the pillow because I w nt them to be handy if I need them during the night. Boots and socks stay by the door.

Unless it is very windy and cold, I leave small vents open at both ends of the tent. Sleeping in a draft or wind will take energy from you, but some ventilation is important.

Information about sleeping bags is helpful. I once thought that down was the best insulation available, but time and experience have changed my mind. Down is great for packing, but it is not as comfortable for sleeping, especially if it gets wet or damp. It takes at least six times longer to dry a down bag than it does a newer, synthetic bag of the same weight. Fiberfill II, Hollofil, Polarguard, etc. retain shape, dry quickly, give protection underneath, and breathe better than down. Dacron 88 is a common bag fill, and it is less expensive than the other fills. However, Dacron 88 does not offer as many advantages as the newer synthetics.

You don't have to spend a lot of money for a sleeping bag. There are many excellent bags for summer use. Bags with two pounds of insulating fill sell for about $40 to $50. I am currently using a Blue Bird made by Slumberjack. It is as good as any I've used. Slumberjack has a wide line of quality bags suitable for most family budgets.

Most dealers will give you a sales pitch for their products. Listen to them; you may learn something. I look for tube construction, coil zippers, a full zipper baffle, and a drawstring at the top. Look at a number of products before buying. Don't buy a mummy bag unless you are positive you can sleep in one; they are too confining for me. You don't need the "ultimate" bag for summer camping. Two pounds of insulation fill will give you a bag with about three pounds finished weight. That will do nicely. Suit the bag to your intended use and not to someone else's.

I used to think a sleeping bag liner was a great addition because I could use it alone on hot nights. However, a flannel liner is bulky, and they shrink like mad. I have tried both nylon and thermal fabric liners. I no longer use a liner. However, a liner will protect the inside of your bag, and you may find that you like one. That is something you have to decide for yourself. The same is true of ground pads.

I am able to sleep quite nicely on mother earth, but you may prefer a ground pad. It should, however, be a closed cell pad, like Ensolite. Open cell pads are like giant sponges; once wet, they stay wet. A closed cell pad about 20 x 40 x 3/8 thick will cushion your shoulders and hips, and it will weigh only about one pound.

I don't have much faith in air mattresses. The cheap plastic ones are notoriously unreliable. But, cheap or expensive, when an air mattress fails in the bush the user is left with nothing. A foam pad is more reliable. There is a trade-off—a pad is bulkier than an air mattress while a good air mattress weighs more than a pad. In some cases your choice may have to reflect bulk versus weight.

The last item is sleepwear. I was born with mine. I will not wear anything I wore during the day in the sleeping bag. Undergarments are slightly damp, and they cause moisture to be held next to the skin. Your body and sleeping bag can function better if the skin is free to breathe evenly.

However, some people get cold easier than others. You could wear a pair of clean, dry socks. Protecting the extremities does help the trunk stay warm. On cool evenings, wearing a T shirt and/or a stocking cap will keep the chill off. A sleeping bag liner adds a few degrees of comfort, and an ensolite pad under you will provide more insulation. In other words, you do not have to buy a new sleeping bag, just add some extra protection.

Cooking Equipment

For groups of six to ten people, I prefer an eight-quart, nested set of pots and pans. I add cups and plates to accommodate everyone in the party, plus two extra cups and plates for measuring and serving. Each cooking pot should have a cover, and the bails should stay in the up position when you want them to. Fry-pan handles should clamp on securely. I don't see any particular advantage in colored aluminum or non-stick coatings for camp use.

My favorite cook kit is made by Mirro for the Boy Scouts of America. The Scout Cook Kit has aluminum plates, which are more compact and easier to keep clean. Partitioned plastic plates, which are more common, are bulky and hard to clean, but they do not cool the food as quickly as aluminum. Additional aluminum plates can be purchased from Mirro, which also offers good kits for smaller groups.

Into voids and spaces in the cook kit I place a 3M Nylon Scrubber and enough forks and spoons for the party, plus two extra of each for serving and spares. I eliminate the knives found in silverware sets because I don't need them. Besides, they are just extra weight. The entire cook kit will hold enough for ten people, including the spare items.

A good cook kit will cost more, but it will last. A cheap kit will warp, leak, and do all sorts of interesting things. It's a waste of money. The Outdoor Living line by Mirro has consistent good quality. I'm still using some of their kits that have seen 15 years of service.

I also carry a cooking utensil kit consisting of: ladle, spatula, long fork, serving spoon, fillet knife, pliers, and tongs for coals. A similar kit with a cloth cover is available from the Boy Scouts of America. It is called the Chef Kit (you would have to switch around some of the items in the kit). It is a good idea to have a leather glove or mitt to use when working around the fire. The utensil kit should roll up so the sharp points fit into the cup of the ladle.

Our camping groups carry one, 2½-gallon folding water jug; one, 2-quart picnic jug for cool drinks; one or two aluminum dutch ovens by BenDonn for baking; and sometimes a griddle if the trip is primarily for fishing. On some 'bush country trips' we camp away from designated sites. Then, it is wise to carry a good backpacker's grill. Those made of stainless steel tubing seem best.

In our food basket I carry the soap bottle, margarine container, seasonings, salt and pepper, and matches in a secure container. One steel wool pad is carried for each day of the trip.

When the weather is dry and burning is prohibited, I carry a two-burner Coleman stove, Model 435 E, though I prefer to cook over wood. The stove and fuel are strapped onto a small, separate pack frame for carrying over portages. The fuel should be enough to provide one fill per day for the stove.

In recent years, I've carried a single-burner Coleman stove on all trips. The stove is carried in an aluminum carrying case, from Coleman. Fuel is carried in one-quart Sigg bottles. This little stove is great for coffee in the morning, and it enables you to cook or make a hot drink even in a downpour. It's become a standard in my regular camping kit.

The last item is a dishpan. Plastic dishpans don't last long in the bush. The best dishpans, so far, are rectangular ones made of stainless steel, available from Sears Roebuck and Montgomery Ward. The dishpans come with a wide rim, not suitable for packing. A sheetmetal shop can trim that and give you a pan with a nice rolled edge. Once you've got that, you've got a dishpan that will withstand years of use.

Cooking Procedures

It is not difficult to organize cooking and cleaning up. When we make camp, the following duties are handed out: (duties last for that evening and the following morning): two people gather wood and tend the fire; two take care of the cooking; two take care of cleaning up; one fetches water. Other members fill in as needed. Using this system, things tend to get done efficiently because everyone has something to do and something to contribute.

Wood: Much of your wood can simply be gathered and then broken. Take only dead wood. Look for a mixture of sizes. Bigger pieces can be sawed up; the axe is not always the most efficient tool. Pine knots, especially from rotted logs, burn well. Use dead branches from the lower parts of balsam fir trees and pieces of loose birch bark for starting the fire. Never strip the bark from live birch trees! Gather an ample supply. Each evening put away and cover enough wood and kindling for the following morning.

Water: Make sure the jugs are kept full in camp while you are cooking. Lake water in the Boundary Waters, at least, is usually safe for drinking. If any doubt exists, water can be made safe by boiling, using pills or a portable treatment rig. Water used in cooking is boiled, rendering it safe. The easiest system seems to be the use of Halzone tablets, which have a long history of effective use.

Cooking: Look over the menu and pull out of the pack basket those items needed for the meal. Soap the outside of the cooking pots completely with liquid soap, such as Basic H. Read instructions, and keep an eye on what you are cooking. In most cases, the cooks should not serve food until everything is ready and everyone is present, but this can be varied to suit conditions. One cook should serve up equal portions to everyone. After that, people may either help themselves or divide up the leftovers.

Clean Up: The dishpan should be prepared with a mixture of soapy water. Each person in the party washes off his own plate, silverware, and cup,which are set aside.

The dishwashers are responsible for cleaning the cooking pots, serving utensils, etc. Usually any lefovers can be burned up in the campfire. When that isn't practical, leftovers can be disposed of by carrying them away. But more on that later. When everything has been washed, the wash water must be disposed of. Then everything is rinsed in clean water, including the utensils washed by each camper. Then repack the cook kit and utensil kit. Leave things in order, and allow the campfire to burn down.

Disposal: This is important. Only organic materials which will decompose should be dumped. This includes food which is not burned and waste water. The waste should be carried away from camp. That requires a short hike, far back from shore. Vermin and insects love food scraps, and you don't want to attract these pests to camp.

A logical disposal spot is a natural depression or cleft. Cover the waste with material from the roots of overturned trees, rotten logs, etc. Do not dig or turn up the soil or tear up large areas of moss. Dumping should never be done near a trail. In some cases, you will need to spread the disposal over two or three likely spots.

I once spent three days on a site that had been 'pigged up' badly by some fishermen. The place stunk, the flies were thick, piles of broken eggs and food scraps were all around the fire area, and dead fish littered the shore and water. We cleaned up the mess, but the ugly memory remains. Proper disposal is important not only to your well being, but to those who follow.

Most designated wilderness and camping areas have some rules. The most common being a can and bottle rule. It is a good rule, one which greatly reduces waste disposal problems. Try to eliminate disposable items, especially those which will not burn, from your pack.

Baking: I usually save the baking until just before dark. It takes about 30 minutes to bake a cake, which makes for a good snack and conversation before turning in. Most snack cakes which require only water will work out fine in a dutch oven. Baking time can be reduced by adding slightly less water than called for or by letting the mix sit for an hour after water has been stirred in. One cake mix in a nine-inch oven will yield six, good-sized pieces of cake.

When you are ready to bake, rake coals out of the fire, but not away from the cooking area. You want the equivalent of six charcoal briquets under the dutch oven and about twice that number on top. Conditions vary, but in about 20 minutes you'll smell cake baking. Check it with the long fork at about that time. If it sticks to the fork, you'll need more baking time. But watch it! The cake will finish baking pretty fast once it begins to look brown on top.

Instant pudding goes real well with a slice of nice, warm cake from the dutch oven. There won't be a shortage of 'appetite' when the cake is ready. Baking is fun, and it is a good evening activity if you've got kids along. You won't have to go looking for them, that's for sure. For some reason, a gray, rainy day can be saved by a nice cake, and even a fine day ends better with a cake to top it off. Baking in camp is a definite plus. Give it a try!

Menus And Food

While camping, you want to eat well because you are active. You want foods that are light in weight but taste good. You do not want them to cost too much. You want things that are easy to prepare, such as entire meals which can be cooked in one pot.

A sample menu at the end of this chapter will give you an idea of the foods I use. But why not create your own menus? Experiment with some meals in your backyard before you head into the bush.

The place to start is the grocery store. See which products can be adapted for camping. In many cases, you can simply repackage the food into plastic bags and add a few ingredients. Your home-packaged meals will cost less than prepared trail foods, and you have more control over what you eat. In addition, I've found that prepared trail foods fall short in filling up a person, and active people need good, filling meals. A commercial trail pack to serve four is enough for three on a canoe trip.

There are a few things which are not usually available in grocery stores. The primary one is Textured Vegetable Protein, referred to as TVP. TVP is the starting point of our evening meals. It tastes as convincing as dehydrated beef, and it is less expensive. I use ½-cup of TVP per person and 1 teaspoon of commercial beef soup base per cup of TVP. This provides a tasty beef substitute, and it is nutritious as well.

You'll also need a good dehydrated egg mix. I prefer Nutri-Egg, which comes in a six-ounce foil pouch and is equivalent to about six eggs. It tastes good (it's excellent with a garnish), but it is tricky to cook the first time. Try this one at home first. It is quite soupy at first, and you need a hot fire to cook it. Nutri-Egg is available from A. J. Pietrus in Sleepy Eye, Minnesota.

At one time I took everything in bulk, measuring out what I needed as I needed it. That saves food packing time, but it isn't good judgment; I learned that the hard way. Now, I select everything for one dish or part of a meal and put those ingredients into clear plastic sacks. I write out the instructions and put them in a second sack along with the first one. Everything is double bagged. I keep each package as small as possible to make it easier to get everything into the pack basket. Sloppy packages are harder to pack. The pack basket has a double trash can liner, so things stay dry and safe. It helps if you pack those meals needed last toward the bottom. *What follows are some specific tips which may help you.*

In planning meals, I try to have two quick breakfasts, such as oatmeal mix, and one evening meal of no-cooking trail food, the commercial type. Those meals can be done up fairly easily on the one-burner Coleman, a great convenience when the weather is nasty. I can usually maintain a fire and cook in a moderate rain, but during downpours, simpler meals are darn handy. If you cook in a light rain, you'll need lots of smaller or split wood. Keep feeding the fire at a steady rate, gradually building up a good base of heat and coals before you start cooking. It's slower, but it works.

Lunches should be cold snacks that require no cooking. Make sure your cups, fruit drink, lunch food, etc. are at the top of a pack. You can organize the pack after breakfast which saves digging through it when you stop for lunch. I carry enough instant soup mix to cook on cold days when we might be forced to stay in camp.

You can make your own munch mix with the following ingredients. Roasted soybeans, peanuts, cashews, M & M Candies, raisins, and sunflower seeds. I figure on using about one-half cup of munch mix per person per day.

Instant puddings work out nicely. I add about 1/3 more powdered milk than is required, which seems to help. Mix the powdered milk and water first. Let it set for a while before adding the pudding mix. The pudding will set up better this way.

Pancake syrup can be made from four cups of brown sugar and two cups hot water. That's enough for five or six people. I have flavored some syrups with Jello, which can be pretty tasty.

I carry coffee, cocoa, sugar, creamer, etc. in bulk containers; one-quart plastic jars work well. Fruit drink mixes are also carried in bulk, but here plastic sacks work better than jars.

I pre-mix garlic salt, pepper, and dill with a complete pancake mix to use as a coating when frying fish. Experiment until you get a taste you like. Dill will make fish less 'fishy.'

You can make an excellent fish chowder by cutting fillets into chunks and cooking them with chicken soup mix and the same seasonings used with the fish coating. Again, experiment to find a taste you like. A hearty chowder is a real boost if you are stuck in camp during bad weather. Kids seem to go for it too.

Margarine is used sparingly because it is hard to get grease off cooking and eating utensils. Stick margarine can be carried in a sealed Tupperware container. Liquid margarine in squeeze bottles is fine, if you pack the bottle upright in the food pack. When margarine or grease is used, clean up is more difficult. Washing twice may be needed. Margarine cannot be refrigerated on the trail, but it will keep for a week unless the weather is very hot.

I apply Basic H to the outside of pots before putting them on the fire. By doing this, soot will wash off easily. Basic H is also good for cutting grease. A 16-ounce bottle is more than enough for a six-day trip. It is a low pollution product, but keep it out of the sunlight because it will begin to break down from light and heat.

It's a good idea to carry one steel scouring pad for each day of a trip. These can be burned after being used.

Meals can be largely vegetarian with good results. Good nutrition is important, but you can't expect the same variety and results you would get at home. Trail food is simpler, but it is fun to cook.

Ingredients for one sample meal.

Beef Stroganoff. Egg noodles, TVP and beef soup base, stroganoff seasoning mix, sour cream mix, powdered milk, salt and pepper. (Most of this comes right from the grocery store.)

Pigeon River Expeditions Menu Sheet

Day 1   Breakfast......... Not supplied

               Lunch .... Cheese, crackers, munch mix, fruit drink.

               Dinner .... Beef and rice dish, cheesecake, fruit drink, milk, coffee.

Day 2   Breakfast......... Oatmeal mix (oatmeal, raisins, almonds, brown sugar), coffee, cocoa, orange drink.

               Lunch .... Sausage, crackers, munch mix, fruit drink.

               Dinner .... Beef stroganoff, pudding, cake, milk, coffee, fruit drink.

Day 3   Breakfast......... Pancakes, syrup, cocoa, milk, orange drink.

               Lunch .... Hard tack, beef jerky, munch mix, fruit drink, candy bars.

               Dinner .... Dumpling stew, pudding, cake, fruit drink, coffee, milk.

Day 4   Breakfast......... Nutri-Egg & garnish, cocoa, coffee, stewed fruit, orange drink.

               Lunch .... Cheese, crackers, munch mix, fruit drink.

               Dinner .... Macaroni & cheese, pudding, cake, milk, fruit drink, coffee.

Day 5   Breakfast......... Pancakes, syrup, cocoa, coffee, milk.

               Lunch .... Hard tack, beef jerky, munch mix, candy bars, fruit drink.

               Dinner .... Scalloped potatoes & beef, pudding, cake, fruit drink, coffee.

Day 6   Breakfast......... Oatmeal mix, cocoa, coffee, orange drink.

               Lunch .... Sausage, crackers, munch mix, fruit drink, candy bars.

               Dinner .... Not supplied.

Note: There is ample food to supply snacks for long days as well as extra fruit drink.

               Pack food for one additional day, just in case.

Packing

Packing skill comes with experience and practice, but a few pointers will help. I use a large pack basket, which holds four pecks, with a canvas cover. I waterproof the basket with two trash can liners. I carry maps under the canvas cover so they are easy to get at. A pack basket carries well, and it is the best container for food. I prefer them to any box pack or sophisticated apparatus. Pack baskets really take a beating, but they hold up because they are flexible. I varnish and go over them every season, and they keep on doing the job. The harness arrangement should be examined before each carry because the harness is prone to slip.

Aside from the pack basket, nearly all other packing is done in the Duluth, No. 3, Cruiser pack, which has a six-inch offset on each side. I prefer the Monarch Brand No. 3 Cruiser made by Duluth Tent and Awning. Their pack is light, roomy, and well made. When packed, the Cruiser is box-like and fairly stable. It will usually stand upright where you set it down. Smaller packs are sometimes used for children, but a child of 10 can usually manage a Cruiser with personal gear.

A day pack may be useful for camera equipment or other items you want to keep separate or handy. I often carry the lunch supplies in a day pack. The pack basket and the Cruiser are roughly the same size and shape when packed. I prefer a number of reasonably sized loads rather than a few big loads or a lot of smaller ones. My packs stow nicely in the space available in a canoe, and they don't shift about. The packing described is meant for effective canoe travel.

Now, let's load up a pack with personal gear. With two people to a tent, I pack their gear in one pack which rides in their canoe. First, in go two, 30-gallon trash can liners. Then, two sleeping bags in 11-gallon sacks. These are stood up, one on each side of the pack. Then, with one arm separating the sleeping bags, I stuff in the small packages of clothes in plastic sacks. I keep pushing them down so the sleeping bags are forced to the outside edges of the pack. Then, I add the two wool jackets in the center space; again pushing them down. I place two packages of towels, etc. on top. The pack is about full, and I can punch it into shape. It should be roughly rectangular.

The flashlight goes into the front pocket. Next, I fold over the trash can liners and tie the two ear flaps. Two rain suits are placed on top of the ear flaps, and then the top flap can be strapped down. If it starts to rain, I can remove the rain suits without opening the entire pack.

A pack loaded this way is stable, and it can get wet on the outside without soaking the contents. In fact, on one occasion we accidently dumped a canoe on a landing at the head of a short rapids. One pack sailed down the chute and was bobbing around below the rapids, but the contents stayed dry.

There is some trick to packing this way. Just remember to use those little dead spaces and push your gear into place, as if stuffing a sleeping bag. Be sure to keep the packages of clothes small; they stuff much easier. Also, if you don't tie off the plasic bags, air trapped in them can escape.

Next comes the equipment packs. In the first one I place three Eureka Timberline tents, standing up. On the back side of the pack I place a ground cloth and the rain tarp, each folded to about 18 inches square. This gives the back of the pack more padding. In front of and between the tents, I work in the pack rod tubes, spinning reels, stake bags, etc. I don't pack the stakes with the tents because of the dirt and sharp points. I work in the load to fill out and shape the pack.

The second equipment pack gets one Timberline tent and the cooking equipment, first aid kit, dutch ovens, toilet paper can, etc. I keep the back of this pack as smooth as possible. The bottom of the dishpan goes against the back of the pack, and the cooking equipment goes into that space. The tent stands alongside the dishpan. With those things in place, I put the three remaining ground cloths and plastic cover at the back of the pack for padding.

Usually, I load up the two equipment packs at the same time, so I can shift things around to get the most efficient and convenient storage for that day. Many of the smaller items, such as clothes pins, lure kits, folding saw, cord bags, folding jug, etc. can easily fill out space in either equipment pack.

If you pack properly, you will have four packs of personal gear, one pack basket of food, and two equipment packs. That's seven packs for four canoes, or a party of eight people. So, you can afford to put the equipment into three packs or carry a few day packs, and still not be overloaded.

Each canoe will usually carry two packs; the personal pack for the two paddlers and one equipment or food pack. It works best if people who paddle together also tent together, but that's not essential.

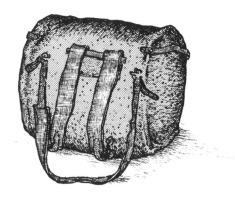

Campsites

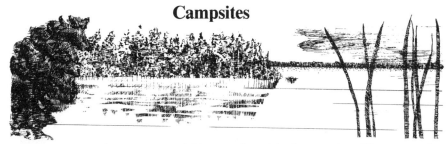

Most campers have a mental image of an ideal campsite. Those aren't common, but good campsites do have some features to look for. A good site has ground cover (grass, strawberry plants, pine needles, etc.) in the tenting areas. A good site takes advantage of the prevailing wind, and is often located on a point or island. A site which catches some wind is less buggy than one on a back bay or river. A good view goes with a good site, especially one that faces an expanse of open water.

The site should be roomy enough so the tents can be put up behind a screen of trees or brush, out of the full force of the wind. I avoid sites that are wide open or park-like. They are pretty, but I dislike getting up in the middle of the night to chase a windblown tent, especially when I'm in it.

It is unfortunate, but the best sites get more than their share of use. Please be careful how you use your campsite.

Some campers look for island sites because they are "safe" from bears. Bears can and do swim; so much for the island theory. I have never been bothered by a large animal. When I was a boy, the first nght I spent in canoe country was on an island. It was a beautiful spot; I was falling in love with the wilderness. But I never got much sleep that night because the island was alive with mice. They had no trouble getting into an old-style canvas tent, and they must have taken great pleasure in dashing across the tops of our sleeping bags.

The little creatures, chipmunks and squirrels included, are more destructive and pesty than bears. So, I keep food out of their reach. Keeping the pack basket closed at night will prevent them from smelling food, so they will probably stay away.

Having spotted a likely campsite from the water, take a look at the shoreline before you land. Careless campers will sometimes throw food scraps in the water. Some fishermen do the same with fish remains. The shore can be pretty foul; if so, it's best to go on. Also, scouting the shoreline will enable you to find the best landing spot.

When you land, secure the canoes but leave the gear in them while you look around. Estimate how many tents the site will hold, and whether the tents will be on ground cover or bare ground. Bare ground sites are over used, and they get messy when it rains. Bare sites often get that way because some campers destroy ground cover by ditching around their tents. Ditching should NEVER be done. If possible, avoid using overused sites.

The next step is to find the latrine trail. Take a look at the latrine. Some campers use them as garbage dumps. Such latrines are often full of maggots or hornets. Latrines are to be used ONLY for human waste.

Look around for firewood. Some sites, especially islands, are stripped bare of wood. Your alternative is to carry wood in from somewhere down the shore.

If the waterfront, ground condition, number of tent spots, latrine, and wood supply check out; start making camp.

People who tent together can begin setting up their tent. Avoid placing tents too close to the fire area because they could be damaged by sparks. Put up your clothesline and start any washing or drying. Tote wood and water to the cooking area.

Establish a likely place to put up the rain tarp, somewhere near the cooking area. The rain tarp need not be put up if the weather isn't threatening. However, it is best to organize your efforts around the place where the tarp would go.

Find two logs, each about four feet long. Place these side by side in the area you've selected. The pack basket and firewood, kindling, etc. is placed on logs so it's kept off the ground. Empty equipment packs and loose gear will go on this pile. Cover all of it with plastic for the night.

Find an area where canoes can be pulled up and secured for the night. Strap life jackets under the seats, stow paddles inside, and turn canoes upside-down, well back from the water. In severe winds, tie the canoes to trees. Canoes should not be left to ride on the water over night.

Cooking equipment can be left outside over night; aluminum isn't hurt by rain or dew. But, make sure the cook kit is together. The axe and saw can also be left out. Loose equipment and anything you don't want to get wet goes on the equipment pile. The first aid kit is placed on top of the pile. The plastic will cover it, but it's still accessible. Make sure everyone knows the location of the first aid kit.

Everyone benefits if you keep things in order and establish simple rules. Equipment left laying around is bound to be stepped on or tripped over. Take the pack rods apart or stand them up in a safe place. As darkness comes, little things like fish hooks become real hazards because they are hard to see and avoid. Keep things orderly; put things away **before** it gets dark.

Since I started camping, I have seen changes in wilderness campsites. Today, in a designated wilderness such as the Boundary Waters Canoe Area Wilderness, you must camp on established sites. These sites have a box latrine and a fire grate, virtually all a wilderness camper needs from a site. Established sites and better camping practices have made a positive difference. In the old days, a wilderness site was often a jumble of abandoned fire rings surrounded by piles of cans and clumps of toilet paper.

Hopefully, those days are behind us. A wilderness camper can, however, still encounter primitive areas where latrines are lacking. A serious camper should know how to properly dispose of solid human waste. Get off the trail, away from the campsite and the water. Find a fallen tree or a big rock. You can sit on a downed tree, and there is usually enough soil in the exposed roots to cover the waste. You could also roll over a big rock, and then replace it when done. It isn't necessary to dig a hole, but solid waste should be covered with moss, rotten wood, soil, etc. Solid waste near the surface, but covered, decomposes quickly because aerobic bacteria work on it.

Toilet paper is a frequent eye-sore around campsites. Too often, a roll of paper will get wet, and then is carelessly tossed aside. We carry spare rolls in plastic sacks. The 'in use roll' goes into a two-pound coffee can with a plastic cover. The can should be sanded, repainted, and clearly marked "TP". (That makes it an acceptable, reusable container in accordance with wilderness rules.)

The "TP" can goes near the top of an equipment pack during the day. In camp, it is kept near the equipment pile. Anyone wishing to use the latrine must first get the "TP" can. If it's not there, then they know the latrine is in use. This procedure works well, and it makes it easier to remember the can when breaking camp.

It's a good idea to place a bar of soap (in a soap holder) under the roll to encourage hand washing. The "TP" can, with it's plastic cover, can be left out over night, but it's best to leave it with the equipment pile.

My last observation has to do with dogs. I like dogs. I like people. Dogs and wilderness can mix if both the dog and its owner are trained. An obedient dog is fine. Take your dog only if you can control behavior such as barking, chasing animals, etc. And please, clean up dog piles around the campsite.

CANOE

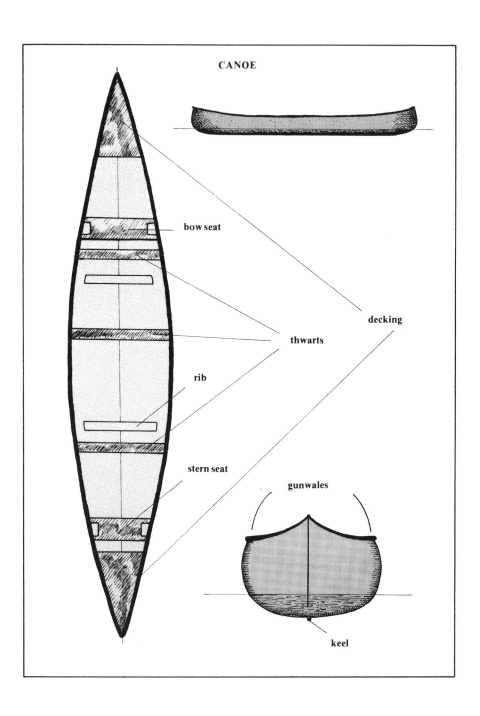

Canoe Handling

The canoe used for portaging and cruising has not changed much over the years. A functional design doesn't need much change. Newer materials have been adapted, and a few design changes are noted, but the basic canoe is familiar to most people. However, let's reaquaint ourselves with some canoe terms before we get into handling.

The sides of the canoe which ride highest above the water are called **gunwales.** Gunwales are usually fitted with a cap or molding to add stiffness to the sides.

A canoe usually has three **thwarts.** These go from one side to the other at gunwale height. They, too, add stiffness and strength. The center thwart serves as the mounting place for the yoke which is used in portaging.

The bottom of the canoe has **ribs.** These are spaced at intervals, cross the centerline, and extend part way up each side.

The **centerline,** which is part of the **keel,** runs down the length of the canoe. The structural parts (gunwales, thwarts, ribs, and keel) are what hold the canoe's shape. I mention this because a safe canoe is a sound canoe. Loose thwarts, a rib that leaks, or a bent keel indicate that a canoe has been abused.

Abuse can be avoided if you understand what holds a canoe together and how to handle it properly. A damaged canoe should not be used until it has been properly repaired. A loose thwart, for example, may not seem important, but it places strain on the entire structure and can lead to further damage. Canoes are safe, but they are safer when properly cared for and treated with respect.

Each end of the canoe should have a small section of **decking.** On newer canoes, the area under the decking is filled with flotation material, so the canoe will float if swamped. There should be a Boating Industry of America (BIA) sticker attached to one flotation chamber. This will tell you the maximum load capacity. However, newer canoes will remain floating when swamped, even with passengers and gear.

The **stern seat** is located close to one section of decking. Decking located behind the stern seat is called the **stern plate.** Decking at the other end is called the **bow plate;** the **bow seat** is located a few feet from it. On newer canoes, bow and stern plates have a rolled edge which is useful for carrying the canoe. On my canoes, I paint the bow plate flat green. This reduces glare and makes paddling in the bow more enjoyable on sunny days. It also helps beginners identify the bow end.

Most canoes have a fixed eye or small clevis where you can tie a rope. The rope is called a painter rope or painter. I have one painter for the bow of each canoe. I tie it off around one thwart when not in use. The painter is particularly useful for quick tie-ups along shore. But, don't leave a canoe rocking on the waves for very long. Aluminum canoes, in particular, can be worn thin after an hour of rubbing against a rock.

That covers most of the terms you'll need to know. Now, let's do some canoe handling.

Maneuvering a canoe on land is easiest if it is right-side-up. Moving a canoe a short distance is easiest with two people, and you'll need to do this at landings and campsites. There is a principle involved, but I'll start by describing the procedure.

First, canoeing partners stand on opposite sides of the canoe, one at the bow, the other at the stern. Partners face the direction they wish to go. They reach down and, with one hand, grasp the canoe where the bow or stern plate meets the gunwale on their side. Now, lift up; the canoe can be carried easily because it will remain level or balanced. If both carriers move one foot toward the center and lift the canoe up by the gunwale, it will still remain level and easy to carry. The principle, then, is to be on opposite sides, the same distance from the ends.

There are times, however, when the canoe must be carried from its center. In that case, the carriers face one another on opposite ends of the center thwart. They bend down and grasp the gunwales with both hands. The hands should be about two feet apart, with the center thwart in the middle. When both lift up, the canoe can be carried in a level position. This is the easiest way to pivot a canoe in tight quarters.

In preparing to leave a landing, the canoe should be carried to the water bow first. But, before setting it on the water, check your equipment. The spare paddle should be tied in. One life vest should be by each seat, and the paddles should be set in. Bring your packs down to the water, close to the canoe.

Now you are ready to start loading. Lift the canoe by its center, and put the bow on the water. Stop when the cargo area reaches the waterline and set the canoe down. While still on shore, load the packs into the cargo area, keeping them on the centerline if possible. Again, lift the canoe from its center, then push the bow further onto the water. Continue feeding the canoe onto the water with a hand-over-hand motion as you grasp the gunwales. Maintain a good grip while doing this. A canoe with its bow in the water and its stern elevated will roll easily.

During this procedure, the canoe is not dragged along the ground. The bow floats on the water as it goes out, and the stern is lifted enough to clear obstacles and prevent dragging. Stop when the stern plate reaches the water line, and set the canoe down. With its stern slightly on shore, the canoe will not drift away, and you are now ready for the paddlers to enter.

The stern paddler must now face the water and sit down on the stern plate in a straddled position. The knees are held firmly against the outside of the canoe. This will stabilize the craft while the bow paddler enters.

The bow paddler steps into the canoe and begins to move forward slowly. The feet stay close to the centerline, the body is kept low or crouched, and arms are spread so the hands can follow the gunwales for better balance. The bow paddler works forward, over the packs, and takes the seat. The bow man must be careful to sit in the center and not lean.

When the bow paddler is seated, the partner in the stern can rise. With the weight off the stern, the canoe will float with the bow down. The stern paddler can maneuver the canoe around submerged obstacles before he gets in. Sometimes the stern paddler has to lift the stern a bit to free the canoe and move it into deeper water. Don't rock a canoe which is stuck. There are times when the bow paddler has to get out so the canoe can be floated to a better spot.

When the stern paddler enters, the stern will settle into the water, and the canoe may ground or become stuck. To reduce that, the stern man should put his left foot on the centerline of the canoe while the right remains on shore. In this half-in half-out position, the object is to get the canoe moving forward before all the weight is in. It's a very quick maneuver, and the trick is to keep your weight with the foot on shore. Sometimes, I simply ease the canoe onto the water until my right foot is the only thing remaining on shore, and then I give a quick push. Your weight should be kept low for better stability. It sounds more complicated than it is. Most people catch on after seeing it done the first time.

Coming into a landing, the procedure is much the same. Approach the landing slowly, and be alert for rocks. When the bow touches shore, the bow paddler steps out slowly, keeping low. He will then sit, straddling the bow plate to stabilize the canoe while the stern paddler works forward as described earlier. The bow man can pull the bow up **slightly** before sitting down, but getting it too high will make the canoe tippy. The stern paddler exits by stepping over one side of the bow.

Both paddlers will then stand opposite of each other by the bow plate. They lift the bow high and walk further onto shore. Stop when the stern begins to drag. If the bow is carried high enough, the cargo area sould be at the waterline. If not, lift the canoe as close to the center as possible, until you can get at the packs. Take the packs out, and carry the empty canoe away from water.

I've spent quite a bit of time on small details. There's a reason for it. If a canoe is going to be tipped over, it will likely happen at a landing. Canoes are not very tippy unless they are hung up on a rock or one end is too high on shore. A great many 'upsets' happen at landings. Maybe people relax too much when they are almost ashore. I don't know. But, I do know that any upset will hamper your trip until you get things dried out again.

Canoe Paddling

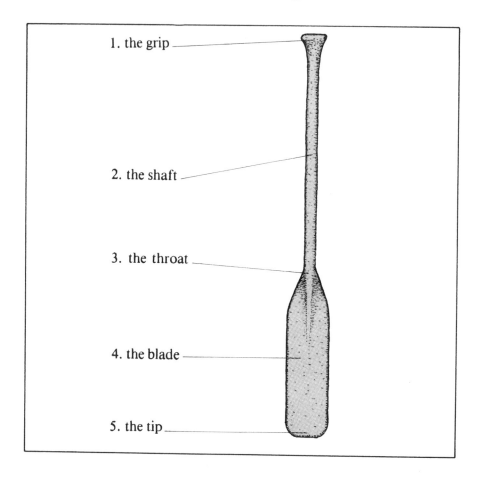

1. the grip

2. the shaft

3. the throat

4. the blade

5. the tip

The paddle is our first consideration. For a beginner, a conventional wooden paddle will work better than a bent-paddle or wide-blade racing type.

The paddle has five parts: 1. the grip—located at the top. 2. the shaft—which runs from the grip to the throat. 3. the throat—where the shaft begins to widen out into the blade. 4. the blade—the broad, flat part of the paddle where your energy is delivered to the water. 5. the tip—the bottom of the blade.

Select a paddle which is about chin high. Paddles come in six-inch increments, so you may have to try two sizes before you find an effective length for you. Heft the paddles that seem right for you and select the lightest ones. Paddles vary considerably in weight, even if they are the same size. A lighter paddle requires less work in paddling.

How you sit in the canoe is important. If you paddle on the left side, the left leg should be tucked under the seat, and the right leg is extended. Do the opposite when you paddle on the right side. Sometimes, I cross both legs under the canoe seat and brace my knees against the gunwales. That provides better stability in rough water, because I ride more with the canoe. It is important to keep your knees down. This improves stability because your weight is lower in the canoe.

When paddling, do not throw your weight around or rock the canoe from side to side. Use your arms and shoulders together to smoothly deliver force to the water. Your shoulders should twist back and forth while the body remains relatively fixed. A little body movement is needed; lean forward at the start of a stroke and back at the end of it. The twisting of the shoulders and slight back and forth movement of the body assists paddling and effectively cancels side to side rocking.

The arm holding the throat of the paddle should be kept straight and used like a lever. The upper arm, the one at the grip, should bend. The lower arm should pull, the upper arm push, and the shoulders swing back and forth with each stroke.

This method of paddling uses a degree of body weight to swing the paddle. It saves muscle energy and makes for more relaxed, rhythmic paddling. There are other styles, but I believe this is best for cruising and for people who are learning to canoe.

As you paddle, slowly increase the force of the pull once the blade is fully in the water. An abrupt pull is hard on you and the paddle. Also, if you allow your hand to ride up from the throat, you may break a paddle by pulling too hard. Force should be applied evenly and smoothly; each paddler should work to achieve that. Study the illustrations in this chapter before you practice. But do practice!

At the end of each stroke, feather the blade by moving both wrists to bring the blade tip parallel to the surface of the water. This is especially important in a head wind. If your strokes are full and reasonably long, you will not have much trouble feathering the blade. The following description covers a stroke with a feathered ending.

Swing forward. As the paddle enters the water, you begin to pull. Increase the pull until the blade is alongside your body. As the blade passes your body decrease pull and begin turning the blade so its **outside edge** will leave the water straight behind you. The hand on the grip does most of the turning, but the lower wrist moves, too. As the blade leaves the water behind you, feather it, and return it quickly to the start for another pull.

A common mistake is to maintain or increase the pull as the blade passes your body. This wastes energy because you are lifting water up. It is important, however, to get a full stroke with a follow-through at the end. The follow-through may seem like wasted motion, but it's really not. The follow-through assists feathering, allows for a brief 'rest' motion in the stroke, and enables body motion to be a continuous flow of movement. It may seem awkward at first, but you will develop efficient paddling. Some rhythm is required, and that comes with practice and experience.

The Strokes

The basic stroke is the *forward or bow stroke*. Put the paddle in the water ahead of you, with the blade at a right-angle to the canoe. The blade follows along the side until it is behind you. Keep your paddle fairly close to the side without banging it. Your lower hand should just be touching the water when the blade passes your body.

The *sweep stroke*. Instead of reaching directly forward, as with the bow stroke, reach forward, but further away from the side of the canoe. Move the paddle in an arc, first away from, and then back toward the canoe. It is a strenuous stroke, and you need not engage the entire blade in the water. The sweep should be performed as a full stroke with a feathered ending.

The *draw stroke*. Reach directly over the side next to your body. The paddle should be at about a 45-degree angle to the water, with the blade entering the water two feet from the canoe. Pull with the lower arm, while the upper arm pushes. Stop the stroke when the paddle is in a vertical position by your side. Feather the blade out as you would do in completing a bow stroke.

The draw stroke can also be done by reaching over the side and pulling with both arms. This method is somewhat quicker, though it requires more effort. A quick, stabbing pull tends to result from this method, while the other favors a long, slow pull. In either case, the canoe will move in the direction of your pull.

I have described the draw stroke done with the paddle moving at a 90-degree angle to the side of the canoe. It can also be done by reaching out at other angles. This is called a *diagonal draw.*

Bow, sweep, and draw strokes can be done forward or reverse. What these strokes do to the canoe depends on which side you are paddling and whether you are in the bow or stern. In general, the strokes have the following effects.

The bow stroke gives mostly forward motion; the sweep stroke side motion; the draw stroke side motion, while the diagonal draw gives forward and side motion. There are times when you can use these strokes in combination, such as starting with a diagonal draw and ending with a bow stroke.

Steering

Steering can be done from the bow or the stern, but under normal conditions the stern paddler steers the canoe. The trick to maintaining a straight course is to look ahead, over the bow of the canoe, at some distant feature.

Move toward that distant point in as straight a line as possible. After a while, it will become second nature. But at first, your attention will wander, and so will your canoe.

In truth, a canoe does not move in a straight line. Paddlers do not paddle with equal force, and wind and waves turn the canoe slightly. A canoe moves through the water with a zig-zag motion. The stern paddler simply keeps the zigs and zags as small as possible.

The Stern Steering Stroke

The *J-stroke* (sometimes called the pry stroke) is the same as the bow stroke **until** the blade is past your body. At that point, while the blade is still in the water, it is turned parallel to the side, just like the bow stroke prior to feathering. But, instead of feathering, use the lower arm to push away from the canoe while the upper arm pulls the grip across your chest.

Some people rest the lower forearm against the gunwale for more leverage. The lower forearm will be well behind your body, with that shoulder twisted back following it. While you pull the grip, straighten your shoulders so body weight can assist your leverage. Feather the paddle when done. The J-stroke is an effective way to straighten the canoe. It can be executed either strongly or lightly, depending on how much turn is needed.

One technical detail about the J-stroke. I have mentioned the importance of follow-through—to let the blade go well past your body at the end of a stroke. This really works to your advantage with the J-stroke. When the paddle is at the end of a stroke, the blade will be very near the stern. In that position, even a slight J is effective for steering. The blade will be close to the centerline of the canoe. The result is a powerful rudder-effect. Even a quick, flicking J, performed as the paddle leaves the water behind you, will be sufficient for many steering corrections.

The J-stroke is essential for solo paddling. If you paddle alone, sit backwards on the bow seat and use the J-stroke. This position puts your weight more toward the center and helps to keep the bow down.

For flatwater or lake canoeing, the bow paddler doesn't have to do much steering. However, at landings and on rivers he can see and avoid obstacles before the stern man—IF he knows what to do.

Bow Steering

On narrow rivers with sharp bends, bow steering is mostly done with draws and sweeps. When entering a sharp right bend, a bow man paddling on the left should sweep once on the left, then switch to do do two or three quick draws on the right. In any sharp turn, your forward motion drops to almost zero, so it's more a matter of pivoting the canoe from both ends and then regaining headway. The stern paddler could either sweep on his right or do a reverse draw on the right to swing his end around.

At landings or on moving water, the *bow rudder* and *cross bow rudder* can be used to avoid obstacles. The bow paddler places the blade in the water ahead of the bow at about a 30-degree angle to the side. The paddler should lean forward and maintain a good grip; there's a lot of force involved. The bow rudders will swing the bow sharply to the side on which the paddle is placed. Meanwhile, the bow paddler should holler out the nature of the obstruction, if possible. (NOTE: The bow rudder is done on the side where the bow man is paddling. The cross bow rudder is executed when, without changing his grip, he must cross the bow to rudder on the opposite side from his paddling.)

Commands

Braking. On command from the stern man, both paddlers slowly lower their blades into the water flat to the direction of travel. **Do it slowly and together!** You shouldn't jam the paddle in the water, doing so risks damage to the paddle or injury to yourself.

The stern paddler should feel free to ask the bow man to draw or sweep as needed, either to maintain course or to maneuver. But make your instructions clear and specific, such a 'draw twice', 'sweep once', or 'paddle harder'. The stern paddler is better able to judge speed, and maneuvering is possible only when you have enough speed or headway. (You should see a path of bubbles off the bow and a whirlpool behind the bow paddle.) Lazy paddling will not get you far, and it reduces pleasure because your work results in little progress. A bit more effort will keep you moving along. Once at speed, you can maintain that speed while paddling with ease and rhythm.

You should be able to paddle on one side for about 15 minutes. I usually let the person in the bow determine which side they want to paddle on and when to switch. A paddler will often develop a favorite side, but it isn't good to paddle on the same side all day. Conversely, switching sides frequently is a waste of time. Frequent switching encourages side to side motion, and the stern paddle drips water into the canoe with each switch. That's particularly annoying for a passenger in the cargo area. In some situations, such as a side wind, the stern paddler must decide which side to use for best control.

Teamwork

All of this "how-to" information will take on more meaning once you try the various strokes. There's a certain 'feel' which comes through practice and experience. Give yourself time to develop good technique.

Remember, paddling requires teamwork. The process of learning involves two people. It can be frustrating for two novice paddlers until they begin getting their signals straight. However, experienced paddlers also go through an adjustment period when they paddle with someone for the first time. Try to be patient with one another during this learning or adjustment period.

Paddlers can benefit by understanding a few simple rules. First, work together. When you launch your canoe, don't start paddling until both are ready. After that, follow a pace and rhythm suitable for both paddlers. Balanced paddling complements the work of both and makes working together productive.

The second rule is to paddle on opposite sides of the canoe. This cancels much side-to-side motion and improves forward movement. There are occasions when both paddlers can paddle on the same side, but it is not standard procedure.

In summary, here's how the different strokes affect the movement of the canoe's bow.

PADDLING ON THE BOW—LEFT
Bow stroke moves the bow to the right.
Sweep stroke moves the bow sharply to the right.
Draw stroke pulls the bow very sharply to the left.

PADDLING ON THE BOW—RIGHT
Bow stroke moves the bow to the left.
Sweep stroke moves the bow sharply to the left.
Draw stroke pulls the bow very sharply to the right.

PADDLING ON THE STERN—LEFT
Bow stroke moves the bow to the right.
Sweep stroke moves the bow sharply to the right.
Draw stroke moves the bow very sharply to the right.
J-stroke will push the bow to the left or begin a left turn if done strong enough.

PADDLING ON THE STERN—RIGHT
Bow stroke moves the bow to the left.
Sweep stroke moves the bow sharply to the left.
Draw stroke moves the bow very sharply to the left.
J-stroke will push the bow to the right or begin a right turn if done strong enough.

When I teach people to paddle, I encourage them to relax—to use their whole body smoothly. Many learned canoeing using another style, the most common being a shorter stroke where the paddle is lifted out when it gets alongside the body. Constant lifting tires the arms, and I'm sure it uses more energy than the longer, swinging stroke. The style of paddling I've described is something people can use day after day with less strain.

Illustrations of Paddling Strokes

Sitting Position 3

Paddling on the right side. Body is centered, left leg extended, right leg tucked under seat. Note position of shoulders.

Draw 1

Paddling on the left side. Sitting position with legs crossed, knees against gunwales. Blade parallel to side of canoe.

Draw 2

Pull blade toward body. Most movement is in lower arm.

Draw 3

Blade is feathered out behind body. Note how upper arm has been dropped forward, ready to start a swing for the next stroke.

Sweep 1

Paddling on left side. Body is centered, right leg extended, left leg tucked under seat. Reach and lean forward, slightly, ahead of body. Blade is at an angle to the side of the canoe.

Sweep 2

Arc the blade toward the stern. Lower arm is well behind body.

Sweep 3

Lower arm completely behind body. Upper arm has dropped. Shoulders are at full twist. Wrists are ready to twist for feathering.

Sweep 4

Blade has been brought out, feathered, and swung forward prior to starting next stroke. Note that both hands are at same level.

Reach forward, well ahead of body. Blade is perpendicular to side of canoe.

Blade is pulled back, following the side of the canoe. Blade stops well behind body. Note change in arm and shoulder positions.

Same as Sweep 4. Blade has been brought out, feathered, and swung forward prior to staring next stroke. Note that both hands are at same level.

Sitting position with legs crossed. Reach forward as in Bow 1.

Same as Bow 2. Blade is pulled back, following the side of the canoe. Blade stops well behind body. Note change in arm and shoulder positions.

At the end of a normal Bow stroke, the blade is left in the water and pushed away from the side of the canoe. The lower arm gives a fulcrum. The upper arm pulls back toward the chest.

Same as Sweep 4. In all feathering out, both wrists are rolled to bring the blade nearly parallel to the surface of the water.

Canoes

The 17-foot, double-ended canoe is the standard for cruising and portaging. I prefer lightweight models with smooth sides. Canoes get faster as they get longer. A shorter canoe may make sense for kids, but it is slower and a bit harder to paddle.

For my use, a canoe with a Bulb T Keel is stronger and does a better job of maintaining course on lakes. There is a lot to canoe design and manufacture, certainly more than I want to discuss here. In terms of paddling characteristics, strength, weight, and cost, I've had excellent results with 15, 17, and 18½-foot, Michi-Craft lightweights. Grumman lightweights are good, too, but Michi-Craft has more features that I like. To the best of my knowledge, these two firms provide the best stock aluminum canoes for wilderness use. Look around for yourself. There are many interesting canoes on the market, but don't get sold on a racing-type if you want a canoe for cruising and portaging in the wilds.

Motors

A motor on a wilderness canoe trip is out of place, completely. Why carry a motor when you can do very well without one? In just 45 minutes, I can teach six people enough to get them paddling fairly well. You don't have to be a super athlete to paddle well, especially with the system I've described. Kids, people who have sedentary jobs, and older people, do just fine with a little help and coaching.

I don't think as many people 'need' a motor as claim to. By not taking an outboard, you'll eliminate a lot of heavy gear, including motors, gas, packboards, motor mounts, etc., not to mention the little 'extras' that sneak in because there's a motor to do the work. And remember, that additional stuff will have to be portaged. I think most groups are better off with a lighter load.

O.K. So I can't change your mind. If you must use a motor, use a square-stern canoe, which is made for an outboard. The square-stern is heavier to carry, and it isn't as well balanced for portaging, but it is seaworthy. A double-ended canoe with a side mount should be your next choice. But that is a tricky rig to control. It isn't stable, and you'll have to go slow and steady until you learn its limits.

Just having a motor doesn't mean you can handle wind and waves better. If it's too rough for paddling, it's too rough for a canoe—PERIOD! Moreover, if you swamp, you canoe will sink by the stern, providing less safety as you bob around in the water. To my way of thinking, a motor isn't a solution to a problem; it's another problem. Use your muscles. It's healthier and safer. You'll be glad you did.

Portaging

I'll never forget my first portage. At the time I was fifteen, traveling with three older, experienced campers. We arrived at the first portage after an hour of paddling. I was casually looking around and enjoying the opportunity to stretch when one of the men called me over. He told me to turn around. Suddenly there was an enormous weight on my back. He spun me around, then deposited another sack on my front. That done, he told me to 'move it', and pointed down the trail. I could barely move! I couldn't even see my feet! Somehow I made it down the trail, but a few thoughts began to form about what is and what isn't fun in wilderness canoe-camping.

The next portage was a repeat of the first, except this time they dropped a canoe over my head and told me to 'move it'. I didn't think anything could be worse than the packs. But, I was wrong! I didn't believe anything could hurt that much for that long without being fatal. I struggled along with a winced face, pretty sure I had found the exact opposite of pleasure.

Looking back, I can see some reasons for my distress. The men didn't prepare me for anything. A 'boy' wasn't supposed to ask questions. I was in the dark about portaging technique, especially the best way to tote a canoe. In those days, too, the equipment was husky stuff, not like today's gear. It was traditional to use the biggest packs on the market, and it was unmanly to have them anything less than completely full. Each pack would weigh-in close to 50 or 60 pounds. Such packs were okay for 'them' to carry, every one of 'them' being 200-pounders. Problem was, I weighed a mere 140. The canoe was a standard weight, 18-footer, tipping the scales at close to 100 pounds. Obviously, I was a bit outclassed when it came time to portage.

I share my story with you to illustrate that portaging can be unpleasant unless you learn some techniques and practice common sense. Fortunately today's camper has better—and lighter—equipment. In addition, most people now realize that portaging is a team effort. Even a little cooperation and helpfulness go a long way to smooth out a rough portage. We can do some things to make portaging more realistic and less of an obstacle.

You see, I'm no giant of the north woods. I'm of average build and weight. The techniques I use are right for me, so they should fit most other people as well. What follows is some information that I hope will turn the 'dreaded portage' into a simple task leading to the next lake and new adventures in the outdoors.

Portage Landings

Most landings are not roomy. I've found it best to have canoes go in one-at-a-time. The first pair should land, unload, clear their equipment off the landing, and be ready to help the next canoe do the same. It works well, and it beats having two canoes jostling for limited space.

As gear is unloaded, carry it up the portage trail a short distance and leave it by the side of the trail—not in it. The same should be done with canoes. The portage trail and landing should be kept as clear as possible, to avoid confusion and a possible mishap from someone stumbling over gear left in the way. Also, getting packs away from the water is good sense. I've seen more than one pack tip over and roll into the drink.

It is likely, too, that another party may be on the same portage, so the trail should be kept clear for them. If another party reaches a portage before you do, wait off-shore until they've had a chance to unload and start portaging. The important thing is to keep an orderly approach that avoids a traffic jam on a narrow trail.

At most portages you will land bow first. Some portages, however, have a rock dome that slants into the water, like a pier. At these, make a side approach. Teamwork is needed on a side approach. If the slope is steep, one person will have to hold the canoe steady while the other unloads packs and carries them to a safe place. Any steep landing requires more caution to unload safely and to get started with the portaging.

Portaging Packs

The best way to move a Cruiser pack for a short distance is to grab it on both sides of the top flap. This is called "grabbing it by the ears." With this grip, you can move the pack easily and lift it high enough to place on

your partner's back. Once he gets an arm through one strap, remove your hand from that side and push up the bottom of the pack. Cooperation in loading packs makes things much easier. The person helping can also check the pack straps to see that they ride flat on his partner's shoulders.

An adult can usually manage two packs over the average portage. An equipment pack should go on the back, and a lighter personal pack on the front. (That's the average load per canoe on a group trip.) 'Double packing', is not difficult, the total weight for two packs is about 40 pounds. It's tricky to see the trail so you have to walk slow and look a bit sideways. You should find that two packs provide better balance than just a single heavy pack on your back.

I advise people to keep their hands free when portaging. It's more comfortable. Besides, it is a nuisance to be constantly shifting hand-held items while you walk. The worst items are full-length fishing poles and the paddles, which either flop around or catch on things. Keeping your hands free, you can use your bandana to wisk away flies as you walk. Of course, it's a good idea to have your repellent handy, too.

Once you start, the best strategy is to keep moving at a moderate pace until the portage is over. Take your time, but keep moving. The average portage is about 15 minutes long, which isn't too bad. Certainly, it's better to have a portage behind you than to drag it out.

It helps to get everything across a portage in one trip. A 15-minute portage will take at least 45 minutes if you have to make another trip. It's not just a matter of time; there is a lot of extra walking and effort involved. You won't be any fresher after making one trip, so try to do it in one shot whenever possible.

Saying that is one thing, but the real world doesn't always cooperate. But, even if people start out double-packing and end up leaving one pack along the trail, you still have gained. Certainly, if someone gets wobbly legs, over-heated, or feels unusual pain, they should rest. When they feel better, they can continue on as before or leave one pack for a return trip. I never rest at the end of a portage if there's equipment behind. I'll slowly walk back, fan my face, and try to cool down. There's no particular hurry, but it helps to keep moving.

For steep or rugged portages, or if the day is hot and humid, I advise people to go slower and do the best they can. Under difficult conditions, double-packing is not expected, primarily because people have to see their feet. If it's been raining, the trails get slick, and tree roots become particularly treacherous. Incidentally, wearing or not wearing a rain suit on a portage is often a toss-up; you'll either get wet from the rain if you don't wear a suit or from condensation inside a suit.

Canoe Portaging

The first step is to prepare the canoe for portaging. I strongly recommend you use a canoe with yoke pads on the center thwart. Don't let anyone tell you to improvise a yoke with canoe paddles. You can do it, but it isn't comfortable—at all! A fixed, commercial yoke will save a lot of grief. It is well worth the cost—an essential item if you plan to portage.

Wedge the two paddles between the front thwart and front seat, or tie them in, one on either side for balance. The spare paddle remains tied to a thwart, as it was. The life jackets should be strapped around the seats. The canoe is now ready to carry, and some potential hand baggage has been eliminated.

The canoe should be carried bow-first in the up-side-down position. The person who will carry the packs should first help his partner get the canoe into an "up" position. Facing the stern, he grabs both gunwales about a foot ahead of the center thwart. Then, he lifts the bow and rolls the canoe over while keeping the stern on the ground. (If you lift too close to the bow the canoe will want to flip over.) Stay toward the center and keep a firm grip. Push the canoe up until your arms are fully extended over your head. The canoe will be up-side-down with its stern resting on the ground.

Once the canoe is raised, the person who will carry it should step under it. He should face the bow, slip under the yoke pads, and extend both arms forward to the gunwales. When the carrier is in position, the person who raised the canoe can lower it to him. The carrier will use his extended arms to hold the bow down and steady the canoe. He should take a few moments to balance the canoe on his body.

It is helpful if the person carrying the packs stays close to the canoe in case help is needed. Teamwork on the trail is important, because the person with the canoe might have trouble unloading it by himself.

Here's some tips to help you carry a canoe. I start a portage with the center of the canoe directly over my head. My arms are extended, and my hands grip the gunwales. I can shift the canoe forward or backward for better balance, mostly needed on hills.

After a while, the weight begins to get uncomfortable. When that happens, I shift the canoe so the right pad is further out on my shoulder, while the left pad rests closer to my neck. I also drop the left arm to give it a rest, or use it to swat mosquitoes. In this position I'm actually a little bit crooked under the canoe, and my right shoulder is thrust forward. When that position becomes uncomfortable, I shift the canoe to the left side. By having three positions for carrying, I can relieve some of the strain and still keep moving.

As long as your legs don't give out, you can keep moving at a decent rate. The discomfort of portaging is mostly due to the weight concentrated on the shoulders. Shifting the canoe is something you will have to experience and practice for yourself, but it is usually done by bouncing the canoe up as you walk.

At the end of the portage, the partner can help unload the canoe. The carrier should, however, lower the stern to the ground by himself, for better control. With the stern down, the partner can step under and take the canoe. He should assume the same position used when the canoe was raised. The carrier then exits. Now the partner lowers the canoe and bends to the side so the canoe can clear his head. With the canoe partly rolled over, it should be lowered close to the body so the weight can be caught on the hip or leg to slow it's descent.

You can unload a canoe alone. With the stern on the ground, grasp the center thwart with one hand on either side of the gunwales. Bend to the side and slowly roll the canoe off your shoulders by dropping one shoulder so it points down. The canoe will roll over, and you should keep the weight close to your body so it can be slowed by your hip or leg.

Portaging is not difficult when there's cooperation and teamwork. A helping hand and a little encouragement go a long way. No one is fond of carrying heavy weights, and it helps if people don't feel all alone in portaging. Teamwork even helps reduce one complaint about aluminum canoes —noise.

The last consideration is attitude. It does no good to feel down about portaging. Make the most of it; after all, it's a break from paddling! Be enthusiastic about your surroundings. Even a longish portage is just about the right length of time for a walk in the woods.

Weather

While camping, you are in intimate contact with the weather. Still it is surprising how little observing people do. You should be aware of weather signs. The most obvious clues are cloud build-ups and wind changes. In bush country, your view is often limited. When you head onto open water, look around to see what may be developing. A cloud build-up and a steady wind in the evening mean you should gather extra firewood and get the rain tarp out. It may be wasted effort, but at least you will be ready.

I have spent entire weeks camping in rain and wind. Sometimes it was so bad we had to stay put, doing whatever we could to maintain interest. It helps to move around, exploring, fishing, or following a hobby. Raw weather places greater demands on the body. More attention should be given to meals and good camping practices. If children are along, it helps to have a simple, waterproof game for them. I enjoy these games myself. The Put-N-Take dice can be used with matches or twigs, for example. Campcraft, such as lashing, or nature study are good, too. The weather is not nearly as clever as your imagination.

If the day is gray and drizzly, you may wish to paddle. A little wind isn't too troublesome. You'll probably end up camping earlier, though it depends on how wet things get. If you are active while wearing rain gear, you'll get wet inside anyway from condensation. Keep your rain gear handy, but wear the wool jacket if you feel cool or damp. Paddling should warm you up, and your body heat will dry your clothes in a light mist or drizzle. Keep warm, and don't let yourself get soaked.

On cold, wet days you use more energy than normal, so be gentle on yourself. Wear a hat; you lose a lot of heat through the head. Your rain gear is important, but sometimes people find out too late that they bought the wrong kind. A temporary rain jacket can be made from a trash can liner with a head-hole in the bottom. It will work for kids, too. Some rainwear claims to be waterproof and breathable, which eliminates condensation. The idea is good, but results are mixed. Apparently these materials are much less effective when soiled or creased.

Usually, rainy weather brings strong winds. Big winds build up big waves. Gusts of wind make controlling the canoe more difficult. The gusts force the canoe sideways to the wind. That puts you into the troughs of the waves—a bad place to be. Aluminum canoes, by virtue of their lightness, are easily turned by the wind, making control difficult. If your canoe is light in the bow, the wind has an even better chance of turning you. In windy weather make very sure your load provides a flat-riding canoe.

In windy weather, canoeists have only two choices: travel with the wind or against it. Paddling into a strong, gusting wind is often a waste of time. It can be done, but is seldom worth the risk. It may take hours to fight your way across a lake that can be paddled in 30 minutes under calm conditions. It is usually better to wait it out, and make up lost time in the evening or the next day.

Going with the wind is easier, but it can be tricky, especially on bigger lakes where waves can build up and gusts get a good shot at you. The danger of going with the wind is that waves can build up dramatically, leaving you no choice but to keep riding with them. Once you are committed in heavy seas, that's it. Turning back is very difficult. In a turn, your canoe will wallow dangerously in the troughs, and a big wave or a strong gust can turn you over. There may be several miles of rough water ahead, and no way to cover it except by hanging on to the canoe. If you see a lot of whitecaps, it is time to be cautious, regardless of which direction you are going.

When waves begin to build dangerously, your best bet is to turn back while you can. Bow and stern paddlers must pivot the craft quickly. Timing helps, so watch for a break in the waves, then make a snappy turn. If you hear the hiss of waves as they pass by at gunwale height, you may have waited too long.

After your turn is completed, you have a long, hard pull into the wind. The bow paddler will get wet from spray, and the canoe may ship water from the bigger waves. **Keep Paddling!** It's no time to stop. Your headway into the wind will be greatly reduced, and control is possible only if you keep moving forward. In this situation, strong gusts are a real problem, and sometimes, you'll be lucky to just hold course.

Consider the following conditions, problems, and strategies:

*You can see the strongest gusts move over the lake because they flatten and blacken the water.

*Waves build up on open water and on the down-wind shore.

*Landforms, such as islands and cliffs, will change the direction of the wind near them.

*Islands and points afford protection from the wind, but they are often difficult to get around in a heavy sea.

*Waves rise up quickly in shallow water. The rise and curl of a wave begins when its bottom begins to drag underwater.

*The biggest waves tend to occur in groups of three.

*Waves tend to bend and turn in toward shore, even when a wind is going down the length of a lake.

*When traveling into the wind, you lose steerage as you lose headway. Control is difficult.

*You can ride safely with your gear in a swamped canoe. Sit flat on the bottom, and ride with the craft. It is also possible to paddle with your hands.

*You must have a life vest for each person in your canoe. Put them on before taking any risks.

*Morning and evening tend to be periods of calm, even on big lakes.

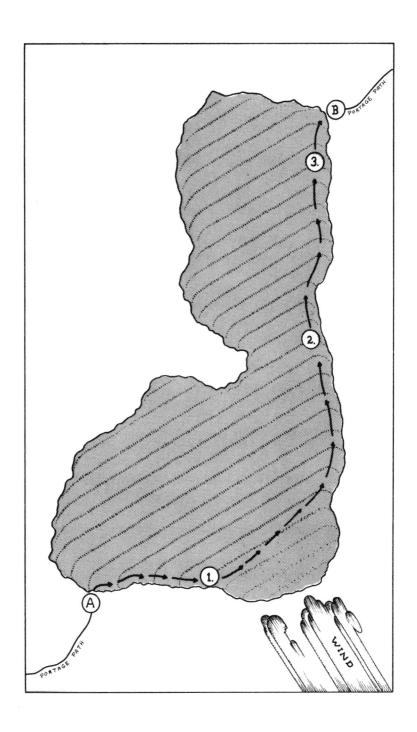

Wind Map

*Most bad storms last a maximum of three days, with calmer stretches thrown in here and there.

*Travel in rough weather should be done in stages, by hopping from spot to spot. A cool, brisk wind, and miles of fighting the waves will lower your reserves. Don't tackle a long, hard stretch if you are already fatigued.

*A canoe in trouble may be difficult to rescue. Keep together; head in or turn back if anyone has difficulty maintaining control. A strong wind can carry tired paddlers into deeper trouble.

***Never** paddle during thunderstorms or lightning.

Look at Wind Map 1. You have just carried the portage and have arrived at Point A. The wind from your right is coming across the lake. The waves are pounding on your landing and along shore. You don't want to go straight across to the channel; the lake is too rough, and you'd be wallowing in the troughs. You have to either paddle or line yourself upwind. If you paddle, the rough part is to get off the landing and get going. The waves will throw the canoe, and water will be shipped in. Load and enter quickly, then paddle hard.

If you line your canoe, attach lines at each end, and walk the canoe up shore. It's a slow process, and you may get wet doing it. 'Lining' is a little simpler if you find two poles (about 12 feet long) and tie one to each end of the canoe.

Note how the the waves turn in toward shore. At Point 1, the wind coming onto the lake flattens out the water before it starts building up waves. Make your turn up toward the channel through that flat-water stretch. It's there, too, that you'd switch from lining to paddling. The waves and wind will be less until you reach Point 2.

Around 2 the wind down the channel is deflected by the land. Also, the point of land projecting into the channel will deflect wind and waves. There may be a complicated wind and wave pattern around the point, depending on the bottom and other features.

You can expect the waves to pile up somewhat in the narrows across from the point. Along the path indicated, you may notice a line of bubbles or foam where the waves begin to turn in toward shore. Your path should be along or very near that line of bubbles. The wind may be strong at Point 3, and you may encounter some large waves. You will be going with them, which helps. Also, the upwind shore will still provide the best protection, and you should be able to make it.

This is a very simple explanation, but it does tell quite a bit about lakes, wind, and waves. If you know how the forces of nature work, you can use these things to your advantage. Imagine your own favorite lakes and how the wind affects them. My example gives only a rough idea of what to expect. A lot depends on local conditions which cannot be shown on a map. Do not over-extend yourself. A cautious decision is better than a foolish one. You can always make up time later.

Remember, heavy seas are nothing to fool with. Things can happen fast, and caution is needed. I'm conservative about travel at such times, because I'm responsible for the safety of a group of people. It is simply not good enough if three out of four canoes make a difficult crossing. Some anticipation of the 'worst' does promote safer planning and procedures.

There are times, however, when a person has no choice but to tackle hazardous conditions. Or, you may get caught in a storm that strikes with awesome swiftness. I hope the following will help you handle such times.

When fighting a heavy sea, it is crucial to keep paddling directly into the wind and waves. It's choppy and the canoe will toss and bounce, but a slight turn can end in swamping. When the bow is bobbing up and down, as in a choppy sea, a larger wave or gust can lift the bow. That allows the bow to be turned easily. It happens very fast, and once it starts you can turn and slide sideways in an instant.

When I see big waves coming toward me, I prepare for them by picking up speed. The bow paddler digs into the tops of the big waves as they approach, pulling hard into them. Paddling in rough water is somewhat restricted because the troughs don't give you much to dig into. Try to make headway in the smaller waves, then ride out the largest ones. It doesn't take long to become physically and emotionally exhausted. The stern paddler will use lots of muscle to maintain course. An experienced paddler has an advantage, but it still takes an awful lot out of a person.

Unfortunately, one cannot always go directly into the waves and wind. When it isn't possible, try to travel as close to a right angle to the waves as you can. In a moderate sea, you can get by that way, but the bow paddler is sure to get soaked. That can be dangerous in itself, if the day is cold.

It's a little easier to run at an angle to wind and waves if the wind is from behind. The wind will want to swing you sideways, but use that to your advantage. As the wind swings you sideways a bit, use a draw or J-stroke to get back on course quickly. You'll find that the wind delivers some energy to your canoe as it swings sideways, increasing your forward speed. In effect, you are using the side of the canoe as a sail. But, a word of caution. Don't get turned sideways too far or you may not be able to recover before you are turned broadside.

Always take side winds into account. To cross long stretches of water, I often head into a side wind for half the distance, and then let it blow with the canoe over the remaining distance. That's not the direct route, and you actually paddle away from your goal before turning back toward it. In moderate side winds, it's best to aim for an area above your goal; the wind will carry you down toward your actual goal as you go.

(NOTE The following is not related to weather but to the rough water of rapids.)

Whether to 'shoot' a rapids or carry the portage is a question that teases many wilderness travelers. Should we do it? I take the portage. It is quicker to run a rapids, but it is a dangerous waste of time if a canoe dumps over with it's gear.

Running a strange rapids is not wise. If you choose to run rapids, you should have whitewater instruction and experience. During a canoe trip, with your gear on board, is not the place to start learning. If you can't resist, however, carry your gear over the portage, examining the rapids from shore, and then run the rapids with an empty canoe. Make sure you wear a life vest which fits snugly to your body.

Wilderness Areas

The word 'wilderness' draws different responses from different people. Some see wilderness as an area of pristine beauty; for others, it is a foolish waste of resources. Some see it as one of a small number of places where people can experience nature; for others, it's an area where they are 'locked out'.

These differing points of view remind me of nature itself. In nature, no single item dominates for long. There is constant shifting back and forth. A dry year is bad for trees, but good for bees. A wet year is good for trees, but it might flood the lakes. The controversy over wilderness seems pretty 'natural' to me.

But, what is a wilderness area? The simplest definition is that it is a roadless area where motor travel is prohibited. It's purpose is to preserve a selected environment for wilderness-style recreation and for scientific and educational purposes.

It's an idea that seems to have caught on. The old days when a traveler was 'alone' in the bush are gone. Wilderness areas are getting much more use. So, you may have to make reservations, even for the largest areas. The pressure is on—all you can do is plan early and act accordingly. For my part, however, I'm glad to see more people interested in experiencing their wilderness heritage.

Wilderness areas are governed by user systems and regulations. Rules are needed because they insure a better wilderness experience for those who enter. The rules have a definite purpose. I urge you to follow them with understanding and concern. If we all bend a little, we can preserve our remaining wild country. Wilderness is not, after all, a renewable resource. Once we develop or abuse it, it is gone. Your cooperation is needed.

Following is a review of the more common wilderness rules.

Controlled Entry. The number of people who can enter a designated wilderness at the same time and place is limited. This distributes "people pressure" and reduces crowding. Also, the number of people in a group is limited to the capacity of the average campsite. This reduces some abuse. A permit for travel is required in most designated wilderness in the U.S. and Canada. This assists the controlled entry program and familiarizes users with the rules.

Motors are prohibited. Human power provides transportation. This promotes the distribution system since people travel at similar rates. The motor ban is less disturbing to wildlife, and the natural effect is improved. The ban also encourages a simpler kind of camping, which turns out to be less costly for users.

Cans and bottles are prohibited. Food containers must be burnable. This has greatly reduced the amount of trash left by campers. Sites no longer look like dumps, and they are easier to keep clean. The earlier approach, which required people to carry out cans and bottles, simply didn't work.

These rules encourage a simple kind of camping which has less impact on the outdoors. Simple, workable camping practices are gentle on the wild country, and they are gentle on you. Use your own muscles and your own spirit to experience the wilds. Most of my customers are surprised by how easy it is, and they seem relieved to discover that, this time, they did get away from it all. A wilderness trip is a human trip, not a high-powered buzz through the woods.

There are several forms of "pollution" I'd like you to notice. One is noise pollution. Sometimes I can hear groups all over a lake. They scream, shout, holler, and in general drown out the quiet. For my part, I like to keep my voice down, so I can hear others and nature. I don't want to make any more noise than I have to, a practice which helps for observing wildlife.

Another form of pollution is visual. Loud-colored tents are a jolt to the eyes. It's called 'distress orange' — it sure is! You don't have to announce your presence on a campsite by looking like an airplane crash. Get back away from the shore. Try to blend in and not mess up the scenery.

The last pollution deals with smoking. In the past, the central area of a campsite was a mosaic of beer caps. Later, the 'pop-top' came along. Today, it's the cigarette filter. Cigarettes with filters should be field-stripped (torn apart) when done. The smoker should carry his filters and burn them at the campfire.

Refrain from smoking while walking or moving through the bush. (In Canada, it is unlawful to do so.) Smoking presents a fire danger, and dry conditions make it worse. Smoke only where it is safe to do so; logical places are by the lakeshore or your campfire.

If you are new to wilderness camping, you may want to hire an outfitter or an outfitter-guide. Look at several who offer such services; ask for a detailed equipment list and menu sheet. A good outfitter can be of real service by taking care of trip details, including planning and permits. An outfitter-guide can make a trip more comfortable and interesting by easing you into things so you don't get hit with the whole load at once. In many areas, guides work under permit or license. Professional help may be just what you need for your first experience.

Wilderness is something I believe in. Over the years, I've seen changes in laws and camping practices that have, by-and-large, been positive. No doubt, there is more to learn and do.

If you think that a wilderness experience is worth having, then I urge you to support wilderness. If it is worth having; it is worth supporting and working for. There are many, active organizations which could use your help. I've been a member of The Wilderness Society since 1960. I support wilderness legislation, preservation, and education as actively as I can. It has been a good experience, and I have learned and grown through my participation. The same benefits can be yours.

Canoe Trip Plans

Planning for a canoe trip is important, yet no plan will ever be perfect. In fact, of all the topics connected with canoe camping, this one is most difficult for me. I know of no plan that guarantees success; but, it's best to have some sort of plan in mind. Remain flexible and keep the emphasis on basic camping.
Here are a few topics which may prove helpful in planning your trip.

Information

State, federal, and provincial government agencies which manage land for recreation can provide route and planning information. Special maps or booklets which cover routes and local conditions are often available for purchase. An outfitter will usually provide information for routing in his locality. Beyond that, a person learns from experience to use an area and adjust to it.

Number of people.

A trip for two people ends up with a slightly greater per-person load. It's not an insurmountable problem, but it is a consideration. Having an odd number of people allows some paddlers to rest, but it is awkward if you use two-person tents. Large groups, more than ten people, are too big to be practical. It's better to have two groups of six rather than one group of 12.

Amount of travel.

A day's average travel for experienced paddlers is 15 miles or better. The first and last days of a trip are often half that average. Less experienced paddlers would be well advised to consider a 10-mile-per-day average.

Consider the following. For a six day trip, allow two and one-half days to travel out and two and one-half days to return. In five days of travel you'll cover 50 miles. One 'extra' day remains for bad weather or just plain loafing.

Even if it's your first trip, try for a 10-mile-per-day average. A canoe trip is a traveling trip, and it is more interesting and enjoyable to travel than to sit on one lake for six days.

If you'll have younger children along, break the day's travel into jumps so youngsters can spend some time out of the canoe. Sitting in a canoe for hours won't work for most children. They need variety and a chance to burn some energy. Even teenagers who paddle well can benefit from a break in the routine.

Time of year.

Just after ice-out, there are usually a few weeks of good, bug-free weather in the north country. The water will be very cold, which creates additional danger. A few weeks after ice-out, the black fly season will start. The hatch lasts about a month. Black flies are most active during daylight hours. When the black flies taper off, the mosquitoes replace them. The early part of mosquito season is difficult.

In the north country, mid-May to the end of June is 'bug season.' This is not a good time for a trip with children. However, fishing is often good then.

July and August are pretty decent months for weather and fewer insects. However, you can expect to encounter deer flies, horse flies, and bees during the warmest weeks of summer. Also, water levels are usually lower. Some rapids may be very shallow or creeks barely passable.

The first cool weather begins toward the end of August. Cool weather means fewer insects; the first frost will dispatch most of them. September and even October are excellent months for canoeing. Again, water levels will be low, and cold water is a hazard. Bad weather during spring or fall is more of a problem, because cold rain—or even snow—can hamper travel. I reduce travel goals by 30 to 40 percent for spring and fall trips.

Clothing for cool weather, spring or fall, should include: Wool cap, long underwear, insulated vest, heavier jacket, gloves, rubber gloves for use while paddling, foam pads for under your sleeping bags, and warm socks. If you use an aluminum canoe, sit on a pad of closed cell foam to reduce heat loss while you paddle.

Goals.

Having a goal is good, but the goal should not get the better of good judgment. Instead of saying, "We are going all the way to Lake X" try the simpler and more realistic "We will try to get to Lake X".

Special interests.

Trips can cater to special interests of people, which is fine as long as camping and basic needs stay in first place. A canoe trip which places fishing or photography first in importance is ill-advised. The fish and scenery will be there for future trips.

Realistic Planning.

As I mentioned, no plan is perfect. Often, we learn by making mistakes—the experience of getting our feet wet. Still, we can learn something from the experience of others. I remember encountering a party on the second day of their wilderness trip. Their story is not unique.

They had left the landing, three miles away, the day before. They were unable to paddle into the wind, so they had walked the canoes along shore. It had been slow, hard work, and they had camped at the first site they found.

Things had not gone smoothly while camping, either. Their equipment was not all they had hoped for. Some of it didn't work properly, and they had not tried it out before leaving home. They also had too much equipment.

They had bought all their equipment at one time. It looked good in the store. But, something that looks good in the store is not always appropriate in the field. They ended up with a lot of "extras" that kept them too busy to enjoy the outdoors. Their canoes were bulging with lanterns, stools, water jugs, stoves, camp sinks, coolers, large tackle boxes, etc.

On their second day, they had paddled some, but things weren't going well. There was an adult in the stern and a child in the bow of each canoe. The bows rode high out of the water, and the wind turned them easily. The group had received no canoeing instruction; steering amounted to ruddering, which gives no forward motion.

They were trying hard to make a go of it, but it seemed to be a tragic adventure. They had been advised to put all their gear in plastic bags. They had done so, placing a large, plastic sack over the **outside** of every pack and bundle. It looked like four people paddling around in search of a garbage dump.

They had simply taken on too much for one outing. They were making progress, and I'm sure they were learning. But, their education was coming at the expense of time to enjoy the canoe country. They would have been well off to back up a bit, to work on basics, and to get their load in order.

Admittedly, having an unwieldy plan happens to experienced campers as well as beginners. I've made similar blunders; it's darn easy to do. Then I graduated to the next step. The first step is to be over-prepared and poorly planned; the next step is to be under-prepared and poorly planned. The reaction is to eliminate equipment, to get down to something spartan. But we usually go too far.

I see this frequently with people who bring only shorts for a canoe trip. They spend a lot of time shivering when it turns cool and rainy. Usually they're trying to eliminate "surplus" weight from their pack. The rain tarp is another victim of "streamlining." It may be dead weight most of the time, but when the rains come, there is no convenient substitute for a good rain tarp to protect the cooking area. It is needed equipment.

Another item people who 'rough it' are inclined to leave behind is the portage yoke. Every time I see someone struggling along with shirts wrapped around a thwart or some such improvisation, I wonder what they are thinking of. A yoke is inexpensive and useful. I am puzzled why people suffer without one.

This back-and-forth movement between being over-prepared and under-prepared may be part of the learning process. I have to keep an eye on myself in order to keep my own plans and equipment simple. It is very human to want to cut corners or be elaborate. After some experience, however, a balance is usually reached.

Experience is always helpful, but it does not guarantee that your planning and preparations will be mistake free. Even the seasoned camper can ignore some obvious detail. I recall a personal adventure; a 1,000-mile **spring** trip to a bird sanctuary on the James Bay in Canada. The area is heavily populated by birds during the **fall** migration. During spring, it has only robins, kildeer, and herring gulls, all of which I can see around my own home. It was an interesting trip, but it could have been much better had I planned my visit for the right season.

Even the best camper will have trouble when faced with unusual local conditions. When the tide goes out on the James Bay, the canoeist is faced with a mile of mud flats before he can get to the water. It was a problem I had been warned of, but actually coping with it was quite another matter. If your timing is off, you may not reach your destination before the tide goes out. Unfortunately, the tide doesn't wait for a person to get caught up. Also, it was on the James Bay that I camped in my first and only sandstorm. It's an unlikely place for such a thing, but nature is full of surprises.

There are many ways for a trip to begin falling apart. If we don't mess up something, then nature will. But you can still take a lesson from nature and use it to shape your attitude for dealing with difficult situations. A trip which has its roots in patience, cooperation, thankfulness, and acceptance will grow in any season.

Even if you get off to a start like the family mentioned earlier, you have at least started. That is something. You'll find plenty of gnarled cedars that started in a poor spot but grew up to become beautiful and unusual trees. We can view trip planning in the same perspective. Experience teaches us in the same way experience causes the cedar to shift its roots to gain a new foothold in life. Our plans may be faulty; our skills may be insufficient, but we can still grow. What we learn from nature and camping can lead to new footholds in life.

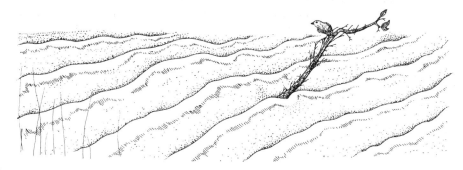

Equipment

Over my 15 years of wilderness camping, I have used and experimented with different types and models of equipment in a variety of outdoor situations. I mention a specific product or brand only if it has proven useful and dependable. I have, by no means, tried and tested all the camping and canoeing products on the market. All I can tell you is what has worked for me—and why.

Each summer, my equipment gets extensive, real-life testing. Many manufacturers produce heavy duty equipment for rental use. The products I mention are **not** 'rental' or outfitter quality; they are all stock, consumer items. You can select from a wide variety of choices; my recommendations are only a guide. I should point out that conditions in the 'north woods' affect my choices. You may have to adjust my recommendations to suit your locality.

Build your equipment kit slowly. First-hand experience will improve your decisions—greatly. Don't rush into buying gear only to find it works best if you camp in the store.

For your first trip or two, you may want to rent what you need. In some respects, renting is more economical than investing in a lot of equipment that will sit idle most of the year. Be sure to ask exactly what kind of sleeping bags, tents, canoes, etc. you will be getting. By asking, and in some cases getting things in writting, you can get the quality of equipment you need.

Following are some additional items on my equipment list which are not detailed in the text.

Life Vest, or Personal Flotation Device (PFD). This should be vest rather than a yoke type, for safety reasons and comfort while paddling. Some firms make vests just for paddling. Closed cell foam flotation, zippered front, and a belt are good features. Make sure it is Coast Guard approved and that it fits properly. Check state and federal laws, but make sure you have a PFD for each person in your party.

Repair Kit. This consits of duct tape and epoxy tape strips carried in a waterproof container.

Canoe Seat. This is a seat designed for use by a passenger in a canoe. The best ones look like miniature lawn chairs that fold. Avoid using a pad or cushion that will hold water.

Rain Tarp. A nylon tarp should have reinforced edges, grommeted corners, and sealed seams. Select a bright color so it can be used as a distress signal. A good size is 10 x 12. Avoid those with tie tapes all over the outside. Pak Foam makes good tarps that are reasonable in cost. Versa-Tarp also makes a good rain tarp; their 12 x 12 is a good choice.

Cordage. I carry one 30-foot and two 15-foot pieces of nylon, parachute-type cord for each tent. This also comes from Pak Foam. I prefer red cord because it is easier for people to see and not walk into. The 30-foot cords are used as extra tie down for tents in severe weather. At other times, the 30 and 15-foot cords are used for clotheslines or camp lashings. The clothesline in each tent can augment your cordage in an emergency situation.

Plastic cover. Plastic sheeting about 6 x 10 feet can be used to cover firewood, equipment, food packs, etc. at night. It can be purchased at lumber and hardware stores. I prefer the clear type, 6 mils in thickness.

Fillet board. This is a piece of ¼-inch waterproof plywood cut to 6 x 13 inches. Don't seal or varnish the surface or it will be too slippery for filleting fish. (That's why I don't use a canoe paddle.) Wash it well after each use. It can also be used for slicing sausage and cheese for lunch. Carry it at the top of the pack basket, along with the maps.

Water jugs. I have used the regular plastic type and the newer 'Water Sacs' which have a nylon shell and a mylar liner. I prefer the 'Water Sac'. It is durable and hardly takes up room. The main difficulty with any folding water container is in filling it. The best way is to take a small pail or even a cup and pour the water in.

Flashlight. One flashlight per tent is sufficient. I carry a spare bulb. Be careful to make the batteries last the trip. The biggest hazard to battery life is leaving the flashlight on by accident, so I reverse the top battery before putting the flashlight in the pack.

Folding saw. The Palco and Sven folding aluminum camp saws are good. They will bend, though, if you are too rough. Keep the blade sharp by filing. Re-set the teeth from time to time.

Stake puller. This is important if you use plastic stakes. With skewers, you can use one skewer to hook into and pull out the others. Don't pull on a tent to get the stakes loose.

Clothespins. I take along 20 spring-loaded clothes-pins. You won't have to chase clothes on windy days with them. These are carried in a ditty bag by Pak Foam.

Pack rods. The Eagle Claw, Trailmaster Series by Wright McGill offers top quality and a wide selection. They hold up under lots of use, and fish well. The metal ferrules and aluminum packing tubes are a real plus for a pack rod. One pack rod per canoe works out pretty well.

Lure kits. I like the Umco, Model P-9, Minibox. It has rounded corners, good catches, a strong design, and ample space. I provide one lure kit for each pack rod. I prefer to pack a number of smaller boxes into the packs than one large one. It's more convenient for fishing and packing.

Equipment Checklist

The checklist is fairly complete, with the exception of personal equipment, which has already been discussed. Obviously, not everything is used on every trip; the list has a range of applications. I encourage the use of a checklist. Once you are in the bush, it's too late to run to the store. Check and recheck each item. Be methodical and take your time; that's good insurance toward a smoother trip. An extra equipment list is included which you can tear out.

ITEM	Needed	Checked	Rechecked
18 ' canoes			
17 ' canoes			
15 ' canoes			
5½ ' paddles			
5 ' paddles			
4½ ' paddles			
Spare paddles			
XL vests			
L vests			
M vests			
S vests			
Infant vests			
Repair kit			
Sail			
Canoe seat			
2 person tents & poles			
4 person tents & poles			
Ground cloths			
Stake sets in bags			
Rain Tarp			
Cordage, long			
Cordage, short			
Flashlights			
Plastic cover			
Sleeping bags			
Sleeping bag liners			
Ensolite pads			
Spare plastic bags			
Sewing kit			
Clothes pins			
Cook Kit			
Plates + 2			

ITEM	Needed	Checked	Rechecked
Cups + 2			
Silverware + 2			
Nylon scrubber			
Chef kit, complete			
Dutch oven			
Reflector oven			
Juice pot			
Water jugs			
Water purifying pills			
Cooking grill			
Griddle			
Fillet board			
Gas stove			
Lantern			
Fuel			
Filter for fuel			
Axe & sheath			
Folding saw			
Stake puller			
TP can			
Match safe			
Sharpening stone			
First Aid Kit			
Liquid soap bottle			
Bar soap & case			
Bastard file			
Pack rods in case			
Spinning reels			
Spin-Cast reels			
Reel boxes or cases			
Lure & tackle kits			
Pack basket & cover			
Cruiser packs			
Map sets			
Compass			
Folding cups			
Field guides			
Other books			
Trip journal			
Misc Items			
Shovel			
Binoculars or scope			

ITEM	Needed	Checked	Rechecked
Camera	___	___	___
Outboard motor	___	___	___
Outboard fuel	___	___	___
Shear pins & tools	___	___	___
Motor mount	___	___	___
Pack frame	___	___	___
Day pack	___	___	___
Children's pack	___	___	___
Canoe pole & duckbill	___	___	___
Bungee cords	___	___	___
Painter lines	___	___	___
Other	___	___	___
Other	___	___	___
Other	___	___	___

Notes

Notes

Equipment Checklist

ITEM	Needed	Checked	Rechecked
18′ canoes			
17′ canoes			
15′ canoes			
5½′ paddles			
5′ paddles			
4½′ paddles			
Spare paddles			
XL vests			
L vests			
M vests			
S vests			
Infant vests			
Repair kit			
Sail			
Canoe seat			
2 person tents & poles			
4 person tents & poles			
Ground cloths			
Stake sets in bags			
Rain Tarp			
Cordage, long			
Cordage, short			
Flashlights			
Plastic cover			
Sleeping bags			
Sleeping bag liners			
Ensolite pads			
Spare plastic bags			
Sewing kit			
Clothes pins			
Cook Kit			
Plates + 2			
Cups + 2			
Silverware + 2			
Nylon scrubber			
Chef kit, complete			
Dutch oven			
Reflector oven			
Juice pot			
Water jugs			
Water purifying pills			
Cooking grill			

ITEM	Needed	Checked	Rechecked
Griddle			
Fillet board			
Gas stove			
Lantern			
Fuel			
Filter for fuel			
Axe & sheath			
Folding saw			
Stake puller			
TP can			
Match safe			
Sharpening stone			
First Aid Kit			
Liquid soap bottle			
Bar soap & case			
Bastard file			
Pack rods in case			
Spinning reels			
Spin-Cast reels			
Reel boxes or cases			
Lure & tackle kits			
Pack basket & cover			
Cruiser packs			
Map sets			
Compass			
Folding cups			
Field guides			
Other books			
Trip journal			
Misc Items			
Shovel			
Binoculars or scope			
Camera			
Outboard motor			
Outboard fuel			
Shear pins & tools			
Motor mount			
Pack frame			
Day pack			
Children's pack			
Canoe pole & duckbill			
Bungee cords			
Painter lines			
Other			
Other			

Tear out copy

90

Into the Bush

Many people have an interest in wilderness camping, but getting started is sometimes difficult. It may seem like an awfully big step. If that's the case, start as close to home as possible. Visit stores that sell equipment, talk with people who go camping, see if some nearby organization offers courses. Things like that, as well as more reading, can be a way of starting. One picks up information and ideas along the way, and there is nothing wrong with starting out small. The process of working up to a wilderness trip is as important and enjoyable as the trip itself.

It may be a good idea to visit an area before you camp there. A stay at a resort is a good way to get a feel for an area and its people. Resorters like people, and can be very helpful. Many times, a long and lasting friendship between vacationers and resort owners is the result.

While in the area, visit historic sites, museums, logging operations, and other sites to familiarize yourself with the general area. The useful tips, information, and familiarity you gain will provide a more confident foundation for future plans. A wilderness trip may be the end result of several years of preparation and experience.

Families with children and senior citizens often seem reluctant to try a wilderness trip. Being away from help can be frightening, but part of that can be overcome if one has friends along. If two families can camp together, there is comfort in numbers, and the work load is shared and lessened. A family with older teenagers can easily include some senior relatives or friends. Children and older people may not contribute as much muscle, but that isn't necessary. We don't have to contribute the same things to be an important part of a trip, or of society for that matter.

It is especially rewarding to travel with a group of mixed ages. People contribute what is appropriate for them at their place in life. Old and young will find they share common values, such as humor, cooperation, and appreciation. In a society which separates old and young so often, it is rewarding to see the generations meet on common ground under the vault of heaven.

There is much to be gained in simple cooperation. Then, as your own skills and experience develop, you may find it enjoyable to share your ability with others who are getting started. Such simple steps lead into the future, a future brightened by the joy of people and the wisdom of wilderness. That's the gift of wilderness, and as we've come to know, the best of gifts increase with giving.

Wilderness does give a gift, part of which is an opportunity. Is it surprising that opportunity will come in the guise of little details? In simplest form, the little details of camping are the fabric of a wilderness trip. The fabric can form a grand design in experience, if details are tended to. If one is tired, wet, and hungry, the details are being skipped and the design shrinks. Simple camping comes first. When that is taken care of, there is time for reflection, enjoyment, and appreciation. Through proper action, the values we hold can be given life.

I'll let a voice as old as wilderness itself speak for me of living values. The Sioux People know this as the Hawk and the Mouse. The Hawk spends his time up high, riding the winds. He has far-reaching vision. He knows where the river flows and what is over the hill. He sees the grand design.

The Mouse is tied to earth. To Mouse, each blade of grass is giant, and he carefully gathers each small seed and fragment to build a nest and larder. The Mouse does not have far-reaching vision, but the smallest detail doesn't escape his notice.

It is obvious, and right, that the Mouse feeds the Hawk. Each flight full of vision by Hawk is fueled by the patient gathering of Mouse. The Mouse and Hawk become One in flight; they join in the cycle of life. It is that way with camping, too. Attention to detail releases the spirit to fly.

This book tries to look at both the Mouse and Hawk. The first part of the book looks after the details; now it is time to observe the flight of the spirit.

Wilderness has a gift. It is not the same gift for each of us. What we are given depends on where we are in life and on what we need to go forward. I do not know where your vision will be directed, nor do I know where your Hawk will fly. But it will take you somewhere. Until your own flight begins, I will tell you about some of mine.

Carrying Place

Follow along on a typical outing with a group of new canoeists. . .

The first day includes some instruction, paddling, and setting up camp, but no portaging. This allows people to get started and to practice basics without having too much thrown at them.

The second day includes two short portages, more paddling, and another night of camping. First exposure to portaging always hits people a bit hard. It is something they are not used to, and it requires more effort than paddling.

On the second evening I tell people that a difficult portage is ahead. We will tackle it first thing in the morning. I tell them: "After the portage, you will know what the word 'portage' really means". They usually ask: 'Well, how long is it?" My answer: "It's 160 rods, but it's not just the length that matters." They usually respond by saying: "We did a 90-rod portage today. The one you're talking about isn't even twice as long, so we should be able to handle it." That's where things rest for the night.

On the third day, within an hour or less of breaking camp, we arrive at the difficult portage. The canoeists act ready and confident to tackle it. I instruct them to go in teams. The portage is a slow, steady climb until just before the end where it drops sharply to the next lake. "Shift the load as you walk," I explain. "When you get overheated, stop and rest until your heart slows and your temperature cools. Use your bandana to mop sweat, to fan, and to keep flies off. We are not in a hurry; take your time and just keep plugging at it. There are canoe rests along the way. When you get to the top the breeze will improve, and you'll have a good view of the lake."

So, off they go. I wait until last so I can check for any gear left at the lower landing. I take my time, but I still pass others. After all, I am used to portaging, and I know how to pace myself on this one. When I get to the end, I unload and then cool off by walking back for another load or to help someone along. There is always something for me to carry, but not because my canoeists are lazy or weak. They are simply not used to carrying loads this way, and their shoulders get tender. Some will get very sore, and leave equipment along the trail as they walk.

Sometimes it takes an hour or better to complete the portage because we have to retrieve so much gear and help so many people. When it's over, the portagers look beat. At the landing I announce: "Well, you did it! That is the worst you can expect. It's done, and now we can go on." I can tell by their faces that what I've said is small consolation. We load up and paddle slowly onto the lake. It takes time for people to rebound after that portage, myself included. However, people who were getting tired of paddling before are now very content to paddle, and being on the lake is refreshing and cool.

After a ten-minute paddle, we break for lunch at the next portage. The little sign says "PORTAGE — 230 rods", and people look concerned. At that point, 230 rods reads like the end of the world. So, I tell them something like this: "This portage is OK. It is a gentle downhill run. It is in good condition, and it is easy. You'll move right along with little trouble. I told you the worst is behind you, and it is. The 160-rod portage is much tougher than this one because of the climb and exertion. This is longer, but it is far easier."

They really don't believe me. They think I'm saying this to humor them into committing suicide. But I remain firm. "We will take everything across in one jump. You know how to manage the loads, so let's do it." On this portage I load up first and take off first. When I get to the end, I unload, and then wait. It doesn't take them long. They are smiling as I help unload their canoes and packs. "Gee, that was easy!" "There's nothing to that one!"

Being a guide does make one aware of human nature. Had I not been there, their plans could have gone awry, and they probably would have searched the maps for a way out with short portages. They would have lost momentum and the desire to go forward, and they would have missed seeing some nice country. I've seen that happen quite often. Many visitors to canoe country flock to routes with short portages. To escape portaging, they crowd together and cheat themselves of a better experience.

The third day is significant because my people come to grips with some important things. They overcame a difficult portage and reached a really nice place. Fewer people, no motorboats, some wildlife—the osprey calls this lake home. That night the canoeists eat well and talk about what has happened. The ground they sleep on is welcome and comfortable. By simply putting one foot in front of the other, they have accomplished a lot. It shows on their faces as they talk around the fire. It was something they did together, and it was worth it.

A person can spend a lot of time and money on 'learning' or 'counseling'. There's nothing wrong with that, but this is another approach. It is a story of life and living compacted into a three-day lesson.

"What if it rains all week?"

Before a canoe trip, people hope for good weather. While we are preparing to leave, I sometimes hear "What if it rains all week?"

To answer that, I'll tell you about Walt, the father, and Walter, his seven-year-old son, because during their week in the wilds it rained daily. Walter loved nature with a direct sort of passion. He couldn't resist living things. Walter would catch and keep everything he could. These 'finds' went into his pockets; worms, crayfish, leeches, bugs. Walt was always checking Walter's pockets and dumping out the wildlife. The cure was temporary; Walter didn't care if his pockets smelled bad.

Walt and I were sitting under the rain tarp. It was raining again. We were hunched over with our backs to the wind while we held cups of coffee and the rain pelted around us. We weren't talking, just sitting. Little Walter came walking along, and Walt called him over. You know how a little boy looks wearing a too-big rainsuit in a rain. It's a tragi-comic look with the warmth of bright eyes and a boyish smile thrown in for balance. "Let me see your pockets." Under protest, Walter complied.

A few semi-living things were released from pocket-captivity, then Walter danced off, looking for more. You just couldn't separate Walter from nature; at least not for long. Walt and I watched him go off, sloshing around in that comical rainsuit. We both chuckled, smiled, and returned to our coffee.

There was a period of silence, punctuated by raindrops falling in coffee. After a while, Walt said: "I'm sure glad I took Walter along. I travel a lot, and I'm real glad to be able to spend some time with him. This is the first time he and I have done anything big together. It's nice. I'm glad he caught that fish. We'll have to go fishing more often." I nodded and listened; I knew this was important, too important for words from me.

The rain kept falling, the tarp flopping in the wind. My coffee was nearly cold, but it was nice to sit there and tend the fire. I got a little more hot water for each of us, and then I returned to my spot. It was miserable out; even with a wool jacket under the rainsuit it was raw. Walt took a sip of coffee, looked at me, and said: "You know, I could get addicted to all of this. I wish it would never end." I knew exactly what he meant.

I've had plenty of trips where it rained and blew a great deal. Sure, it was raw and cold at times, but we still found enjoyment. We watched the rain move down the lake in sheets. We saw clouds roll and cover the sky with enormous patterns. We watched the quiet mists skim over the trees or move like clouds over the water. It was beautiful, because what was right for the land was also right for us. We drank in the spectacle and its meaning like the trees and plants drank up the water.

The rain slowed us down and changed our plans. But, we had good times, good conversation, and good spirits because the joy of life knows the joy of rain and of green life.

It's not logical. But, something in us transcends logic, and if it comes to a person in a rain storm, or as the sun sets after a difficult day, the important thing is that it came. It brought a measure of peace and understanding. Here in the wilderness, we suddenly **know** why the birds sing so sweet.

From a Low Cliff Looking West

On the Minnesota-Ontario border, there is a lake the French Voyageurs called Lac Original. At its eastern end there is a low cliff that affords a view to the west. It is not a spectacular cliff, only 15 feet above the water, but I like to go there every so often to camp and enjoy the perspective.

Where the cliff ends to the southeast, there is a portage. It starts in a natural break in the cliff. It's such a convenient break that it looks like it was made. Nature provided the start of the portage, but the trail was made by man.

The portage connects two lakes, but it also connects us to the past. By recent estimates, about 12,000 years of human activity have passed this way. But, we don't really know that much. We can identify some typical artifacts from cultural groups, but much still escapes us. Part of the trail is elusive.

At times I've wondered how we compare with an older culture that lived over much of the upper Great Lakes as far west as Manitoba. Its people made decorated pottery and beautiful stone tools. They worked deposits of native copper, and their trade lines sent copper far to the south. Their culture lasted for 800 to 1,000 years. Will we last as long? Will there be purpose and beauty visible in the remains of our civilization? The questions make me pause.

Part of the reason I come here is to look for evidence that weathers out of the ground each season. The bits I find go to a repository in Canada, where the work of many people comes together. I'm glad to be part of that effort. But, in doing that work, a person can't help but ponder, and wonder, and feel. I hold a piece of nicely worked stone, and I feel I know these people and a little of what they were like. I have enough in common with them to appreciate what they have left behind. These scant remains speak for those who have gone before.

Maybe the land taught the early people about peace, acceptance, and balance. Their work displays awareness. Their legends are a treasure of the new world. In legend and myth, the collective wisdom of a people has survived. It speaks as eloquently as nature itself. It is a quiet message that, if we can bring ourselves to listen, may be what we need to alter our present course.

Even a little understanding of those who were here before helps me to better understand myself, of where I am strong, of where I am weak. Faint whispers from the past add perspective to my life. The view from this low cliff reaches further than I can understand. It reaches toward the heart of things, and there, knowledge blends into feeling and so gains direction. The connection to the past becomes real.

Part of that perspective involves getting here. You must portage to get here. It's just difficult enough to make people want to find an easier way, but there is no easier way. In fact, the physical burden of portaging is a relief compared to some of the burdens we've added to life.

Faced with so many options, decisions, and choices, do we become so busy that we lose the pulse of life? Not so on a portage. You feel a portage directly. You either press on or you stop and look for an easier way. Going on will get you to the goal; trying to out-smart it will leave you where you were. Reality is that blunt. Money, education, connections, achievement means nothing here. Putting one foot in front of the other is the language of success.

This ancient portage is a link with the past and a lesson for today. Our destination is another view of life, of the world. It is not a perfect, theoretical world, but what point of debate or logic does one need with trees, sunlight, water? Mental gymnastics do not alter our relationship with the land. Like the portage itself, we have grown from the earth.

This portage is a link between lakes, between times, between peoples, between man and nature. Indeed, the trail may be broad enough to be a link between man and God. The view from this low cliff is more than I can understand, but it is not too much for me to accept.

I heard nature drumming
on an island late at night,
on top of Agawa Rock,
at the Height of Land in a waterspout.
I heard the drumming,
the three 'Thunders' of the native people,
trying to waken my spirit,
but I didn't listen.
I went back to corridors and work,
to do what was expected and secure.
I didn't listen,
until the drumming moved inside,
almost tearing me apart;
the drumming of change,
'Change Or Die'.
I choose to live with my spirit
in the Upper Country
where my spirit reaches out.
With sureness and freedom
I reach out to you.
The wings of my vision
touch gently around you,
so gently you may not notice
my humble drumming for you.

Foggy Morning

When I left the tent that morning, I found a dense fog surrounding the lake. It was chilly and damp after the previous night's rain. I could just make out the shoreline about 30 feet away, and the sound of my movement seemed to hang in the air like the fog.

I was the first one up, so I moved quietly. I heard, before I saw them, two gulls lift off from the sandy shallows. Their wings beat against the heavy air with a soft whump, whump, whump. The gulls, white shadows in a fog that swirled with their passing, flew low over the water. They headed west, across the channel, and were soon gone from sight. I stood there, listening to their invisible passage for what seemed like a long time.

I uncovered the kindling, twisted the twigs into a tight mass, and laid out birch bark. I took my time because on a wet morning you have to build up enough heat for a good fire. The twigs and branches made surprisingly loud snaps and cracks as I broke them. The smoke and fog was a continuous cloud around me. Nothing moved. It all hung there: dead air and dead smoke.

The fire was going well enough, so I soaped up the coffee pot, filled it, and set it on the fire. There was nothing else to do until the others awakened, so I cooked coffee, and watched the fog.

The fog was thinnest from the ground to about three feet up. I tried to look at things from that level, but it didn't help much. Then I remembered the gulls. They hadn't flown up; they had stayed low over the water. Maybe that was their way of coping with the poor visibility. I could imagine the problems of a bird trying to fly in a fog; there was nothing to go by. The gulls were lucky. They could fly low over the water, and if they tired or became confused, could just plop down on the water to rest.

The others were starting to emerge from their tents. It was time for breakfast. It's funny how weather effects people. The group was pretty quiet. They huddled around, and breakfast was a low-key affair. By 9 we were pretty well done with eating and packing, but it was slow going. We tried to dry the tents as best we could. I had stopped paying attention to the fog, but it was still there, and the day was warming up. By 10 it was lifting a bit, and I could see the tops of the spruces across the channel 30 yards away.

When we started to paddle, the fog was burning off more quickly. It was starting to feel hot and very humid. By the time we reached the creek to the first unnamed lake, it was a clear, sunny day. It was good weather for the last day of a trip, and the fog was almost forgotten.

Wildlife Story

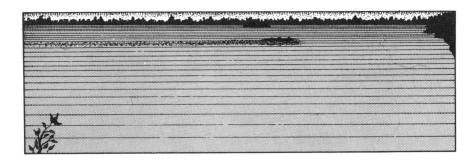

People enjoy the comedy of nature. The antics of a chipmunk in camp are sure to bring a smile. People are moved by the drama of nature. One of my groups, bold teenagers, was left in awe at the way an otter harvested ducklings on the river. A life and death struggle happened before their eyes. People ponder over the mystery of nature. This story is about something unexpected.

I had reached Bemar Lake on the east side of Quetico Park. It was little more than an hour before dark. The shadows were long, visibility was limited, and the clouds were low and ominous when we headed out from the portage. Our destination was an island where we intended to camp. We could see a stand of red pines on the island as we paddled. I remember thinking that we were lucky to be close to a campsite after putting in a long day.

We were about halfway to the island when we saw something ahead in the water. It didn't look like anything I had ever seen before. It was too big for a beaver, and the shape was wrong for any of the larger animals.

We stopped paddling to study the creature. As we watched, it turned and started swimming toward us. I wanted to stay put, to see what it was, but I don't like to provoke or interfere with wildlife. The best action was to paddle sharply away from it; that would show we were not attacking. As we paddled, we heard a bleating sound—like a moose calf. I was puzzled. I knew something that big shouldn't bleat like that.

After we steered away, the thing turned and we could see it broadside. Whatever it was, it was big. It looked about eight feet long. There was a long hump in the front, a smaller lump about three feet behind the first, and a third hump, the largest, about four feet behind the second. As it swam, it continued to bleat—like a moose calf.

Whatever it was, it had our interest. We shadowed it, while the creature bleated and swam, slowly heading for shore. We moved in closer as it neared shore. It started to splash and began to climb out of the water.

To our surprise, it was a cow moose, but one with a large hump on its back. Then, as the cow stood knee-deep in water and mud, the hump jumped off. The hump, a moose calf, landed alongside the cow, and the two of them clambered up the bank.

The moose calf had been riding on her back. The extra weight kept the cow's body submerged except for the head. That made the calf look bigger than she was. Then, too, the calf was fawn colored, not the dark brown of a mature moose. All in all, it turned out to be a pretty good disguise for a cow moose.

The cow stood looking at us from the bank. Maybe she was appreciating her trick. More likely, she was giving her calf a chance to take cover. Finally she turned and followed the calf behind the trees. They disappeared into the bush, but the mystery was solved.

Somewhere they are drumming,
in the aspens on the river,
among pines on the ridge,
in deep sphagnum bogs.
You are the walker here,
mind-playing with many things,
walking, automatically, lost in thought.
Then, thimbleberries and ferns,
with the smell of earth-life,
will stop you standing,
while the drummers drum
something for your soul.

Fall Portage

Where there's a rapids and falls, the portage is steep. I was carrying the canoe, and the climb hurt. A canoe is torture in a steep climb. It's weight bounces against you with every step, and you have to struggle to maintain balance. After a while, it gets to feel like a gigantic headache. All you can do is keep going to the upper landing.

That could have been the end of it, but this time there were sacks of wild rice to carry. As I walked back, I thought about things that were eating at me. The weight inside me was as heavy as the weight I had just carried. I've told myself, many times, to enjoy what I've got when I've got it. But this time I didn't or couldn't, and my thoughts tried to drown out the hiss and roar of the water in the gorge below.

So, I felt bad going both ways. Fall is a sad time for me, anyway. There had been no frost, but some of the trees had already changed color. Summer was dying. In one spot the yellow-brown birch leaves covered the mud of the trail, nature's version of the golden road. It was a nice symbol, but it wasn't enough to cheer me.

Then it happened. At the top of a rise, I was greeted by the smell of fall: ripe perfume rich with birch and alder, cool mists, browning grasses. I can't describe the smell of the autumn forest, but for me it was like having the blanket of the universe enfold my soul and hold it quietly. I knew where I was because I knew what was there with me.

I continued down to the lower landing where my companion was loading up. I knew, then, I could give him my joy, very neatly, like a leaf on the water.

The Road of Travel

Before you begin, look at yourself.
You are unprotected; no fur, no claws.
Your canoe is small, your skill lacking;
you are noisy when you should be still.
Take kinikinik, before you start,
and give it to the water with your hopes.
Do that quietly, and be sincere.
Later, you may leave more kinikinik
at a special place.
You will know the place,
and you will leave something there.

The berries that go into pancakes
deserve to be thanked for their being.
The fish you catch when needed,
is worthy of thanks for all fishes.
The winds are full of fliers;
let your thoughts join them in thanks.

You know the right manner
for the road of travel.
It will take you to the road of life.

Labrador Tea

The Labrador tea plant is typical of the northwoods. It grows widely, wherever there is enough moisture. It's a scraggly, low-growing bush with narrow leaves that are white and fuzzy on the underside. You'll often find it in bogs, but sometimes it grows on rocky outcrops along with blueberries and wintergreen. The leaves can be used to make a distinctive drink.

I begin by gathering branches with their leaves attached. I cut off only one or two branches per bush. When I have a bundle of branches, I tie the stems together and hang them in a warm place to dry.

I don't bother with the branches again until several weeks have passed. Then, I shake the bundle vigorously, to get the dead spiders out. Next, I begin picking the leaves, letting them fall on a piece of newspaper. A lot of little dusty stuff falls off, too, but it's easy to separate from the leaves. Last, I put the leaves in a jar.

To prepare the drink you need some time. It's not instant. I take about twelve, medium-sized leaves for each cup of tea. I heat an appropriate amount of water, and turn the heat off when the water boils. Then I add the leaves, allowing them to sit in the water for a quarter-hour. I reheat the water until it begins to boil; then I shut the heat off as before.

It takes a while for the brew to get up to strength. You may have to experiment to find the strength you like. I have let larger batches sit on the stove for a day or more, and the brew just gets more and more woodsy. (You may wish to add more water.)

Blueberry leaves, wintergreen leaves and berries, strawberry leaves, etc. can be mixed with Labrador tea; that makes a nice drink, too. But straight Labrador tea is the drink I prefer.

There is no other drink like it. It's the north country in a cup. The woman who taught me about it had her first cup in a wigwam years ago. She said: "You've got to coax it out of the leaves." She was right, but it's worth the effort.

Sleep

Toward morning, you'll start to rouse. The first light of day is registering, and the birds are starting up. I'm sure that one feels and hears morning coming unconsciously, before we actually wake up.

Once up, it is time for a fire, some coffee, something to eat. Then, break camp, pack, and get ready to paddle the next few lakes.

Paddling takes some energy and concentration, but it leaves the eyes free to roam. The mind does likewise.

Noon is a good time for a break, something to eat, and a bit of a rest. After that the paddling begins again, and the rhythm and flow pick up as one moves along.

Later in the afternoon, the paddling begins to slow. It's more of an effort. A swim would be nice, but it is time to establish a new camp, split wood, then maybe take a quick dip.

After you have eaten and cleaned up around camp, you can feel the difference. The wind has calmed and there is just a hint of coolness in the air. The loons start to call and a few birds fly low over the water as the shadows lengthen and night advances. The dark holds the shore first; and the lake remains illuminated til last. It happens slowly and with beauty. After the day's activities, it's time to relax, to watch the night come, to talk with your companions.

One of the finest things about wilderness canoeing is learning how a day ends. We live in such a compelling electric environment that we often miss it. The lights burn, and after the 10 PM news we realize it is time to sleep. Then, we hurry off to bed, as if being tired had to occur on schedule.

In the outdoors, we are prepared for sleep little by little. Our day ends with a degree of calm and relaxation that is seldom found after watching the latest bad news on TV. I can't think of a better way to head toward sleep than to be gently moved toward rest by the spectacle of sunset.

The campers feel it, too. It's like they have stepped into a new relationship with life. It shows as they are drawn around the campfire before turning in. I've sat around many, many such fires. It's always the same, and yet, it's always new. Matt will tell a joke. Jess falls off his end of a log. Laura sits in Joy's lap while her hair is brushed. Missy watches the glowing end of a twig. Brian makes plans to do some morning fishing. Lisa keeps her journal. Someone is thirsty, someone else yawns. What happens around the fire is a timeless, human picture.

Later, in their minds, they will return to this time over the years. It becomes a rock of recognition. Something as transitory as day's end becomes a focus of understanding.

After sharing the warm glow of the campfire, the campers face the trip to the tent. They leave the safe circle of light. The dark is strange. The black cloak of night that hangs in the trees may bring fears. After all, this is a strange place for most people. Even the word 'wilderness' suggests some wild and fearsome place.

The simplest way to banish such fear is to substitute appreciation and thankfulness for it. These positive feelings slowly nibble away at fear, and, in time, they leave peace as large as sunset.

A hungry bear will not walk out of the woods. There is very little in a well-kept campsite to attract a bear. Certainly, nylon and aluminum isn't bear-food. You'd have to wear fish as earrings before a bear would give you close, personal attention, and even that might not work. But, for some reason, the bear is a frequent symbol of nighttime fears.

We experience fear over such things, but reality teaches that our sleep is more easily distrubed by the whine of a single mosquito than it will ever be disturbed by a real bear. The bear we fear is the one we imagine. It's the bear we don't see, but think about, that gives us grief. It is the bear of fear and inexperience that haunts those mental woods.

Fears are real, but they are not reality. The slow coming of night, the loons, the long shadows, the chill of the air, and purple and gold sunset, the drone of mosquitoes. . .these things are the reality, and these things are easy enough to live with. When you sleep in the wilderness, you sleep in the lap of creation. It is our mother earth and our first home, full of good news and beauty. If we set aside fears from civilization, we will soon feel at peace.

How To Lure A Bear Into Camp

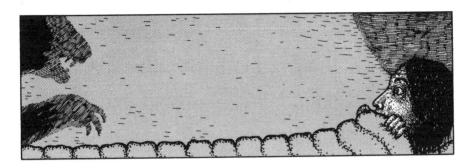

Some of the more frequent questions from campers concern bears. So...in a lighter vain, here are some of the bear facts.

For years, I have seen youth camp guides wearing a leather gizmo on neck or wrist. Finally, I had an opportunity to ask one of them what it was. He told me it was a 'bear scare' and went on to give some hazy explanation of how it worked. It sounded like a hoax, but I filed the information for the future.

Some folks have another form of 'bear scare'. It's an empty, one-gallon steel can with 20 to 30 quarter sized rocks in it. When shook, it makes quite a bit of racket. At night, the camper with one of these needs only to shake it, and bears will be scared off. The person sharing the same tent will be a nervous wreck, and the whole group will be slowly edging toward oblivion from lack of sleep. But, they won't be bothered by bears, or if they were, they'd be too tired to care.

There is another bear scare that is milder. It's done mostly at night. It goes with the words "What's that? Did you hear something?" The object is to wake up someone else and have them scare the bear. If you are a sound sleeper, you may know the variation of this called, "Are you awake?" A sharp poke is followed by "Are you awake?", as if getting kicked in the ribs would put you to sleep.

The ultimate form of bear scare is the sidearm, various forms of the .45 being preferred. The person with one of these has it made. When they hear a strange noise at night, they calmly roll over, grab the weapon, and fire off two rounds into the air. It's best if they don't share a tent with someone with a weak heart. The first round will wake them up with eyes wide open. The flash of the second and its report will convince them that their maker has come, for sure.

The more adventuresome sidearm users will go outside before banging off a few rounds. You'll know when they do it because you'll see flashlight beams spearing the night immediately afterward. Next, you'll hear a speech something like: "Everything's OK. I heard something, but I scared it off. It's OK now. Sure glad I got this gun along. Go back to sleep now, everything's OK." I've written this down for you, because at the time it's being said it's hard to hear over the beating of your heart.

In a few moments, the person outside will decide that he'd better stand guard for a while, in case the thing comes back. This is called 'natural guard duty'. The subsequent shufflings, thumpings, wood splitting, and coffee pot jangling will coincide with your dozing-off periods. The heavy sighs coming from the one standing guard mean he would like someone to guard the bushes with him.

Don't do it! The desperation of the situation makes it tempting, but you'll only get a re-hash of the entire episode. You'll get plenty enough of that in coming days, and after the second or third time, it is about as welcome as a mosquito bite on the lip.

You can see how much fun the average false alarm is. It's even more fun if there really is a bear, and that brings us to the 'meat' of luring a bear into camp. Without a real bear, the bear scares are only momentary diversions.

First, you have to select your location carefully. You want a lake which has road access and which is used frequently by canoeists, day-campers, picnickers, and fishermen. They pave the way, and without them, it's kind of a bust.

When you have the right location, then it's a matter of finding the right time and place. It's best if you show up in August, that way the above-mentioned people have had a couple of months to prepare the ground-work.

The site has the following characteristics. The fire grate shows signs of hamburger frying and hot-dog roasting. It should be greasy looking, and with luck, fragments of hamburger or hot-dog have escaped being completely burned up. The smell of such things is a main ingredient in the bear lure.

The area should show signs of food scraps. What picnicker could resist the cute chipmunk? A few little pieces are tossed when they first show up, but before people leave, they'll feed the critters. Why let these buns go to waste? You're in luck if you see most of a bun or bread slice in the area.

Next, go look at the latrine. If the others have been doing the right kind of work, it will be nearly full with sacks of garbage. To a bear, that gives the site the appeal of a garbage dump, and who's to say the bear is wrong?

Sometimes, the garbage has been left out in the open, apparently for the trash man to get on Thursday. The sack is tied at the top, but small critters have made some holes, the ravens have picked bigger holes, and the wind did the rest. Greasy paper plates, tin foil with lots of hamburger juice, onion peels, and bread crusts—all have done their bit to spice up the lure. Incidently, in evaluating the quality of the lure, look for an empty mustard jar and some beer cans. Both are good signs and indicate a high quality lure.

You've hit the jackpot if someone cleaned fish on shore and left the innards close by. Bears like fish; that's one of the best lures. The only thing better is fried fish. With any luck at all, the grease and smell of fish from a shore lunch has worked itself into the lure.

You're off to a good start, but you're not home yet. The odds are in your favor, but it's time for a clincher or two.

You need to carry fresh meat for the first night. Get some juice from that on the ground, and leave the freezer paper unburned by the firegrate. As much grease as possible should be spilled into and around the fire. Grilled steak smells good to a bear, much better than hamburger.

Also, catch about four fish. Clean them just before dark, so you're not inclined to get rid of the innards till morning. Who wants to stumble around near dusk while carrying a bear's favorite food in the bushes? So, leave the innards for morning. Two of the fish must be fried. Use a roaring fire. That scorches your pan, releasing more tantalizing aromas. Eating fish in the dark will result in a few pieces being dropped. See how easily a good plan fills out?

Save the other two fish for breakfast. They'll keep overnight, and the odor will add to the lure overnight. That scorched, greasy fry pan is too hard to clean in the dark, so just put a little water in it, and let it soak by the fire.

You've now done all that is humanly possible to lure a bear. The only thing to trip you up is if someone else has done a slightly better job nearby. If that happens, you have to extend your lure into the next day.

If your lure goes into the next day, simply continue the base you've built. For breakfast, by all means fry bacon. It's greasy, hard to clean, and smells wonderful to a bear. Get the grease spread around. Use real eggs, too, and make sure the shells aren't completely burned up after breakfast. Leave a few dirty pans for later and use the time to catch more fish for tonight. Remember to keep forgetting to dispose of the innards.

Have smoked sausage for lunch, and don't burn the wrapper or casing. Work it into the lure someplace or other. Then do all the things you did the night before, and your bear is bound to show up.

The point behind all of this is that you have to **work** to get a bear into camp. If you don't do the right things, well, you just won't get one, unless by accident.

I have never been bothered by a bear, and I don't intend to be bothered by one. I've seen plenty—around my house in the fall, along roads, at the garbage dump, etc. I've only seen a couple in the bush, and then not for long. By not packing fresh meat, bacon, etc., and substituting all dry food, well there's just not much to attract a bear, unless he's bored or craves TVP. The camping practices I use don't give a bear much of a target, either, so I go on year after year missing out on the fun.

The Time of Things

In a cedar paddle, an ash pack basket,
a canvas pack, there is time past.
When I paddle, I want the good cedar
to touch the water for me.
I want those things to know one another,
and myself,
in a movement of unity.
The aluminum, nylon, and plastic
are in unity with something else,
which has its time now.
But, when I touch the water
to move,
to give direction to my course,
I want the good cedar there
to speak for me.
The cedar and water
are one, together,
in the right manner.
That is what I need.

Spirit World

When the spirit is strong in the land, it grows strong in those who love the land. Those who lived here first knew there was more to the land than geography. The meaning of their legends is sometimes unclear, but the feeling in them is undiminished.

The legends tell of two youth who were close and two serpents who were rivals. The serpents wanted to know which one had the stronger venom, and so, each snake struck one of the youths. The Natawa Snake brought death into the world when the youth he struck died. For this, he was banished to live under the water. It is a story men know in many forms.

They tell us how Grandfather Bear broke through the four layers of the Earth to bring us to this place. Our Grandfather brought us here to live, because this is a good place. This is home.

They tell us how men should live together, and they warn us how difficult that is. There have been many sad incidents in the growth of The People, and there have been incidents where The People lived well on their road. There are incidents, too, which show that those who honor and respect their Source are pleasing to the world and capable of great sacrifice and great humanity.

The vision of the world is cloudy and confusing until you step into the Spirit World and follow the old and true road for men. That is a great accomplishment for anyone humble enough to begin it.

They tell us, too, how the Megis Shell led the People from the east to the west; how and why they stopped to rest, and the names of their resting places. The road behind is graced with names given by The People in their passing. It is a good road, and full of meaning.

The Megis was last seen at the western end of Lake Superior. The sun reflected from it in glory, surrounding The People, and then the Megis was gone. The road for men continues, but men now travel without the direct guidance of the Megis. Men must use what they have been shown and given.

Legends such as these touch the heart. There, they touch the human core. Those who love the land know, from the heart, the meaning of legend.

Windbound

A friend and I had been on an exploration trip back in the bush. For days we had been travelling on unnamed lakes, creeks, and beaver ponds. Our portages were mostly game trails, and finding some of them had been a challenge. We were covering a part of Canada that doesn't get much use. Our goal was the Border Route where we'd connect with the more heavily-used routes.

We had just finished our last bush portage, a one-mile affair used mostly by moose, and we were looking forward to some easier going. The portage came out on a deep, sheltered bay. It was about a quarter-mile to the main body of the lake, where the water looked choppy. We had noticed the 'breeze' as we crossed some high domes of rock on the portage, and it seemed pretty 'breezy' even here in the bay. But, this was no place to linger, so we moved on.

We were coming out near the middle of the lake, and it looked rough. In the narrow mouth of the bay, we studied the waves while our canoe rolled in the swells that curved into the bay. It looked as if we could sneak our way up into the wind and use the curve of the shoreline as protection. That's what we did, for about a half-mile. But, it was just too rough. Before we lost what shelter we had, we turned toward shore and found a campsite. The site was high, and it had a poor landing, but it was a lot calmer than the lake.

We set up camp, and by the time we were settled in, some black clouds were coming our way. We gathered wood, secured the tent better, and ate a quicker-than-usual meal. Then the first rain began. When it's blowing and raining, there's not much to do but crawl inside the tent and wait. We talked and killed time.

The rain let up shortly before dark. We went outside to look things over. There was no end to the clouds, and the sun was setting behind an ominous-looking sky. After doing a few chores, we turned in.

By first light I was awake. I looked outside, but it didn't look encouraging. But, you never can tell, so we made a quick breakfast, and then 'partially' prepared to break camp. I say 'partially' because it didn't look promising. It wasn't, either. In less than an hour we were forced back into the tent by a driving rain.

Around mid-morning the rain let up, but the wind seemed to be increasing. Inside the tent, we waited and rested. The tent, however, was restless. Suddenly, it made a leap as the stakes on one side tore free, allowing the tent to rise and begin to roll. That woke me up! When it settled back, we scrambled out to set things in order. The tent was fine, though we had to re-set the stakes and add additional tie-downs. The tent would stay put, but it was taking a beating.

As long as we were outside, and not a bit tired, we decided to go inland and explore. We took some lunch and off we went. Not far away, we found a passage in the rocks. It was about as wide as a car, and the walls were near 10 feet high. Put a roof on it, and you could turn it into a garage. We tromped around for nearly two hours. Then the sun started to show, so we went back to camp.

The sun was shining nicely, but the wind was still strong. The lake looked as wild as it had earlier. It wasn't long before the sun was blocked out by an in-coming squall, and once again we ended up inside the tent.

By late afternoon the weather seemed much worse. We put our rainsuits on and went outside to stretch. It was then that we saw the waterspout. It didn't look like much at first, just a swirl on the lake that made a hissing sound. It got larger and moved in rapid, jerky jumps over the surface. It passed in front of us, then turned and disappeared into the bay we had paddled through the day before.

The funnel was so fascinating that we just stood there and watched it. But once it was gone, we both looked in the direction of the rock passage for safety. In the same moment, a flash of fear had us wondering if a spout had passed earlier when the tent was lifted. Had a funnel passed even closer without us knowing it?

The rain increased again, so we returned to the tent. Now that we couldn't see any danger approaching, our ears searched for warning. It's not very relaxing to sit in a tent and jump at every strange sound. Also, I was getting sore from so much sitting. But, the rain kept hammering down, so we stayed put.

A few hours before dark the rain slacked enough so we could cook a meal. It's difficult building a fire when it's windy, and cooking is more tedious because the wind blows the heat away. At least it was something to do that didn't involve sitting. It was a treat to be able to do camp chores and move around, but it didn't last long. Shortly before dark the rain began again, and more wind came with it. Reluctantly, we headed back into the tent where we sat while it got dark and the rain poured down. It kept up all night, and I slept fitfully, at best.

By morning I was anxious to get out of the tent. Conditions were improved, but it was still windy. We studied the situation and agreed that we had to get off this shore while we could. Being pinned down was getting to us.

Skipping breakfast, we broke camp in 20 minutes, and we were off. Unfortunately, as we broke camp a new squall arrived. We were soon paddling into a stinging rain driven by mighty gusts of wind. We went about one mile before we had to give it up. We turned toward a clearing on shore where we had to haul our cooking gear and food far back to get out of the wind.

We ate breakfast and watched the waves crash on the shore below us. Neither of us wanted to put up the tent. That was just too painful a thought. So, we sat under the trees in our rainsuits and waited. I remember how happy we had been to start paddling that morning, but we were grim and sombre as we waited.

In a situation like ours, things can deteriorate. A person can experience extreme rage over something minor. It is human to want to scream or cry; it may even help, but it doesn't change anything. Maybe nature sensed that we had enough. By noon it had calmed somewhat, and we were able to paddle away from that exposed shore. We had a tough pull into the wind, but I don't think I've enjoyed paddling as much as I did that day, not in a long time.

Carry it with you

What you gain in wilderness
is always there, waiting.
It was myself, very sick,
who gave up hope
in the hospital, alone.
The death-wish growing
and the whispers of wildness
not strong enough to cure,
just strong enough to heal.
For weeks I stayed,
barely holding my own way
while the whispers continued.
What causes the spirit
to be reborn? To grow?
The quiet wildness was there,
waiting to grow with me,
waiting to give freely.
'Accept and give it all.'
the spirit said;
'Give it away, give it away.'
The storm outside
lashed my window,
and I watched the skies
give their waters away.
Carry it with you,
and give it away.

Unnamed Lake

Longer canoe trips, especially in Canada, will take you through at least one unnamed lake. To me, these quiet, secluded places are special. Seldom do they have a campsite. They are not spectacular, like the big lakes. They are humble places. Their shores are often dark bogs of stunted black spruce which form a wall of hanging moss and lacy branches.

I feel wonder and appreciation in these places. There is something stark and photographic in the drowned trees that stand deeply weathered in the black water. There is subtle beauty in tall reeds and grasses, green-gold at the margin. Most of these lakes have an outcrop of white granite somewhere along the shore. The rock slants up from the water to gleam in the sun like a bare bone of the earth-skeleton. The gleam always seems to be there, connecting the unnamed lake to the larger universe.

How clear and sharp is nature's picture. The grand vistas provide superb viewing. But often I recall, even more vividly, the smaller fragments passed along the way. In the simplest and humblest way the message becomes clear. A blue-dead crayfish in the shallows shows the cycle of life. I see only that end of it, but I sense the larger picture.

I am often tempted to establish a permanent camp on some unnamed lake, so I could watch its life. I'd like to see the lake slowly dry along its edges in fall. I wonder if ducks use this lake during migration. How many muskrats work its shore before winter? I would like to see it freeze over, the ice forming a white field that cracks and groans through the deep-cold nights. There would be tracks in the snow, each telling a story written in winter's language.

I would like to see the approach of spring begin with the softening of the deep snow. The first black spots would appear on the ice, then, ice-out. The lake is fluid again, and life picks up along its edge. In the deep shade back from shore, some snow would linger until May. But, in a few weeks, summer would claim all. Summer would see a few of us pass through, though we would keep moving, probably looking for something grander.

I have much in common with such places. I want to linger where the watershed is more my size and scope. I can feel at home. My own life can be that basic and real. Living well in nature is peace and health. It is my world and life, and it reminds me of where I came from and how it was that I arrived.

The unnamed lake is not alone, nor is it unimporant. It is connected to other waters. It is part of wilderness. It is part of all life. In my heart, there is the joy of recognition.

Beaver Pond

On most canoe trips we take at least one nature hike. Follow along as we head into beaver country. . . .

Our hike starts where a creek enters the lake. We hike up stream through an area of balsam, cedar, and ash. This part of the forest is gloomy. You can see where high water floods the shore. These floods destroy much of the smaller growth. What survives grows large, and the trail twists around massive trunks of trees.

In a short distance, we reach a clearing. At first, the remains of a beaver dam are not visible, but they are there. The center of the dam has been washed away, only the wings remain. The mind's eye can imagine how the dam backed up water. Dead trees, now standing on land, had been drowned. The larger ones have nest holes. Even in death the trees are part of life here.

The creek is not big, two leaps and you'd be across. But, the valley is large. Nature has done a lot of carving here. The beaver picked a good place for a dam. I can imagine the old days, when small creeks were a chain of ponds that flashed in the sun like jewels.

Our path continues. We climb gradually. Around us are the toppled trunks of aspen harvested by long-gone beaver. The trunks and stumps are weathered. The remains blend into the land, much as the pond was once part of the valley.

The climb gets steeper. From up here, you can see how far the beaver's work extended. But, from this new vantage point we also see a change in the land. The trees are different. On the highest ground, the trees are White, Red, and Jack Pines—all fire species. Living trees and the remains of others show scars from past fires. Many forces have shaped the land we see.

We hike through high, level ground. Here, the creek has cut a canyon with steep sides, and there are two falls. Beyond them, we begin to approach another beaver dam, one that is still in use.

As you come closer, move quietly. You never know what you'll see. Sometimes it's a beaver, but it might be ducks, or a heron, or even an osprey riding the winds above us. The pond attracts many creatures. Even if we don't see any, there is a flat muddy area where they leave a partial record. We've seen tracks from moose, fisher, mink, weasel, mice & voles, shrews, and lots of birds.

At its highest, the dam is a little over four feet, but it's long and spans the valley. On the dam, there is one spot that's used by some bird or animal which leaves behind a pile of crayfish shells. The dry side of the dam is often a nesting site for ground hornets. We don't look for them; they find us, and then everyone scatters, avoiding that spot.

But even the hornets can't detract from the beauty. The pond is a living jewel. The marsh grass is rich green. The channel twists through the center of the pond like a silver serpent. It's a peaceful scene, and yet it's bursting with growing things and life.

You just have to stand there for a while to appreciate how the wind makes patterns in the swaying reeds and how ripples catch the sun in the channel.

After surveying the scene, look down into the water. In the still water, you can see insects moving. Schools of minnows flash past. Larger minnows dart around the vegetation. Snails cling to stems. The more you look, the more you'll see. I've been here many times, and there is always something I didn't notice before.

Last summer, a biologist interested in the wilderness area took a canoe trip with me. We were standing on the dam and talking. He was looking into the water, when he bent down and began to examine something that looked, to me, like an algae bloom. It wasn't. He explained that it was a large colony of bryozoan. My expression was blank, and he went on to explain that bryozoan require a stable, clean environment. They also filter water in the process of extracting their food. He said: "The water in this pond is of good quality or the bryozoan wouldn't be here."

His enthusiasm was something else. Aquatic biology was his main interest, so he was in heaven. Much of the detail was lost on me, but not the enthusiasm and sincerity. I didn't have to be a biologist to recognize the importance of what he said. What he described left an impression.

It got me thinking. I had never thought of a beaver pond as contributing to water quality. Yet, from what he said, it looked as if the pond was acting like a natural water treatment plant. I began to wonder if I wasn't missing the importance of other contributions from this pond.

Some of it was obvious. Every trip to the pond resulted in more contact with wildlife and wildlife sign than any other place during the trip. The pond had to be making a contribution to the wildlife community. The beaver's contribution to that part of the environment seemed large.

As I thought more, it occured to me that the ponds might fill a gap missing in our deep, cold lakes. The lakes have very little shallow area, so the ponds fill in that part of the food chain. Instead of seeing two things—a pond and a lake—I saw one thing, an aquatic community. In that sense, the contribution of the beaver ponds seems crucial, at least to me.

Since that time, I've continued to think about the beaver's contribution. There's much more than I have time for now.

At times, I've been amused by the way some 'scientist' would go into a rapture over something I thought was minor. In this case, I thank creation for the enthusiasm of my biologist friend. He has helped to start me down a productive trail.

Even in history the beaver has been important. The fur trade is evidence of that. The beaver were plentiful then, and they were the cause of much early exploration and development. In a way, it was the trail of the beaver we followed to our present course. There are even cities that grew as the result of fur trading posts. It's quite a story.

In time, we exhausted the resource, and beaver became scarce. They were so profitable that we didn't know when to quit, until we were forced to. I have nothing against trapping, but if I had to pick between a live beaver or a fur, I know which one I'd choose.

Spring

When I was a kid, I'd plant
two or three lima beans
every spring.
I'd put them in the window,
and every day
I'd water and watch.
That was a sign of spring.
I just had to plant those beans,
every spring,
for many years.

Almost any spring day now,
I'll be working outside
in the cool, damp air.
The sun will feel warm,
and there will be a little
winter in the shade
and under the trees.
It will happen any day, now.
I'll be working
when I hear them coming.

They come over the big lake.
Their voices speak
of going home, of going north.
The big V of Canada geese
will come over with voices
calling from deep inside.
I'll stop what I'm doing
because for a little while
I have to be up there
with them, going north.

No body is too old or young
not to understand that.
The work just has to stop,
and I feel like celebrating
the beauty and mystery
that flies over my head,
going home to the north
for another season.
What I feel
is no dumb accident of nature,
and neither are those geese.

Peace

It was the last day of the trip. We were camped on a site where a sand spit curved into the lake. After we ate, Bobby wanted to hear 'The Frozen Logger' one more time. It's a fun song, and I sang it for him again. After a few times, the kids knew the words, and they anticipated the funny parts. It didn't take them long to make the song their friend.

Then, Bobby asked for some Naniboujou stories. Naniboujou is a mythical character, a super-hero in Ojibway legend. He always bounces back, but he has the same human failings as the rest of us. When I tell the legends, I get as much out of it as the kids. The stories still do what they did for centuries. Through words we rejoin an ancient tradition.

Toward the end of a trip, the canoeists are soaking in as much as they can. There is something different in their faces and voices. They feel moved to speak even as they try to hold onto each fleeting impression.

At the end of the lake, the big cliff picks up the glow of the setting sun. It is serene, yet awesome in its beauty. We look at it together and feel the same thing. There is no need for speech.

It is a time for being at peace. It comes after a few days—people feel more at home and relaxed with life in the bush. The strangeness and doubts are gone, and sitting around the campfire with friends represents as much of the world as they need or want to know.

It is peaceful. The kids are played out after their romp in the water. They bargained with mom and dad to be able to 'skinny swim', just this once. They ran, played, splashed, and were as close to being natural as they could get. Now they are tired and content to rest.

There is a lot going on around the little fire, but it goes on inside us. It shows in our manner. The last day on the trail has special meaning, and it is not unusual for us to linger on after dark. The conversation takes many turns, but it often returns to nature.

We talk about the land—its history and its beauty. There are many faces to the land, and each person finds a view that suits their place in life. Its meaning is a personal thing; each has his own interpretation. But, inside we feel the same union with nature. It is almost mystical. The mind follows a path as bright and clear as the moon's reflection on the water.

The peace of nature is, of course, only passing. Nature can be harsh, but being close to it makes one aware of the larger reality. We know that nature renews itself; life continues to grow. The next day will be new, and each day is part of the universe and of our part in it.

We know that nature does not storm or burn to confound us. There is nothing antagonistic in it. The real peace is a feeling of being in touch with the world and all that is in it. Peace is an internal realization that we are part of the whole. With that comes an acceptance of the cycles and drama of life.

So, the night deepens, and before we turn in, there is time to look up at the sky. The path we followed for a week has brought us to this place and this time. This day began with a blaze of sun rays and bird song; it closes with a personal view of the stars.

Campfire

It was a little after dark.
Paul said, "Let's have coffee."
Add wood to the coals,
get the fire burning,
put the water there to heat.
Just that simple,
a few people by a fire
talking in the golden light.
The heat feels good
in the evening cool.
One of the nicest fish
we've ever caught
came in today.
We talk about tomorrow,
we laugh over today
with a cup of coffee
and a few people
around a fire.
It's just a fish.
It's just some instant coffee.
It's only a little fire.
But try telling that
to your heart
while your eyes reflect
the golden light
and the stars
are white diamonds
above you.

Loon Call

The north country is loon country, and the loon's haunting call rings through that timeless space we call wilderness.

There are stories about loons. An older fisherman on Lake Superior told me about catching loons in gill nets set in twenty fathoms of water. Often, the loons were not drowned, and once brought aboard, they fought wildly, fouling the net. He told me he hated it when he caught a loon. His face and voice confirmed the tragedy he spoke of.

A native from Canada told me about dancing loons. When she was a girl, the loons would gather in the morning near her camp. By pairs, they would dance across the water, each pair taking its turn, like a courtship dance. After the ritual was over, the pairs would leave for their fishing areas. She didn't know for sure, but her thought was that as the number of boats on the lake increased, the loons stopped their morning dance.

I have always noticed loons; they are strikingly beautiful on the water. Still, I took them for granted until a few years ago. I was paddling down Northern Light Lake one evening, following a long arm of the lake past bays, islands, and points. The lake was a beautiful calm path, leading us along. It had been a good day, and it was a fine evening.

Off to my right was a pair of loons. They often allow canoeists to get fairly close, so there was nothing unusual about the closeness of the birds. One bird started to call—a slow, wailing cry with longer notes than the loon's laughing call. The sound hung in the air like something rare and personal. It really struck me. My partner and I stopped paddling. It was the first time either of us had heard a loon call at close quarters.

A loon call is not easy to describe. It is a sad, beautiful sound that haunts dreams and can't be duplicated. One loon, probably the male, gave the long echoing call three times; I could almost follow the sound across the lake and into the distance.

We drifted in silence after the loon finished its third call. But I was still listening. About three quarters of a mile away, another loon picked up the call and repeated it. We could see the loon and its mate resting off an island in the distance. The call from that pair was the same as the one we had just heard, but the increased distance made it less commanding.

After the second pair was done answering, another pair picked up the call somewhere behind us. Gradually, the sound was passed along from pair to pair as the day turned toward night. The sound became part of the dark shadows along shore. It drifted into the purpling light of evening and the slowly-gathering mists. Some of the calls were very faint and far away; others were close. Sometimes two calls would mingle in evening music. It was the stuff of dreams and visions. It was the loon voice rejoicing in wildness.

Readers with knowledge of animal behavior will recognize what I've described as a territorial display. The call and spacing of the loon pairs seem to indicate that each pair claims territory for fishing or nesting. But, I hope you will see beyond that to the beauty of the loon voice joining the night.

It took me some time to move from hearing the loon to understanding it. My memory of the loon call was teaching me something. In my mind, the loon was no longer a 'lower animal'; it was representative of life. Slowly, I began to see the life of the loon as equal to my own and having instruction for me. What I learned made me feel frustrated. Why wasn't my own life as simple as that of a loon? Why did I continue to place knowledge over life and living.

Observe: Each spring loons mate and nest. They care for their nest and its contents during spring storms and cold. They defend it. They are busy and often hard pressed by circumstance. Raising young is no glorious, intellectual dream; it is a daily task with frequent frustrations, sacrifices, and defeats. But the loon doesn't worry over such things. It doesn't let knowledge, pride, or rights interfere with its being. The loon survives against odds that would drive most humans to collapse. It doesn't put anything, no matter how glorious or impressive, over just being a loon.

Think how many birds mate for life. Think how many people advance to 'freedoms' which leave their nests shattered by a storm or abandoned for a new attraction. A loon succeeds by sticking to what it is; a human fails by trying to be what he's not.

Often I have noticed that people close to nature live by a natural reaction. They gather food when it is ready. They enjoy friends when friends come to visit. They are happy with the little things in life. They don't have a reason for liking you. They accept all that life has to offer, and they accept pain and suffering with as much certainty as anything else. In accepting what is, they share in the wisdom of the loon.

I am no philosopher. But I am stirred by my memory of that evening when the loons called near my canoe. The shadows grew longer, the air began to purple and dim toward night. The lake and land accepted and reflected the coming of night. In the rising mists the loon calls echoed and repeated as one canoe with two travellers paused and then continued on.

That experience is past, but my soul and spirit remember and are renewed. I learned something from my brother, the loon, that can never be taken from me. I know that I do not preserve the wilderness; it preserves me.